RTHUR MILLE

T

roken Glass

—

commentary and notes by
AN ACKERMAN

s Editor: Enoch Brater

METHUEN DRAMA

Methuen Drama Student Edition

10 9 8 7 6 5 4 3 2 1

This edition first published in the United Kingdom in 2011 by
Methuen Drama
A & C Black Publishers Limited
36 Soho Square
London W1D 3QY
www.methuendrama.com

Chronology of Arthur Miller by Enoch Brater, with grateful thanks to the Arthur Miller Society for permission to draw on their 'Brief Chronology of Arthur Miller's Life and Works'

A CIP catalogue record for this book is available from the British Library

ISBN 978 1 408 12884 8

Commentary and notes typeset by SX Composing DTP, Rayleigh, Essex
Playtext typeset by Country Setting, Kingsdown, Kent
Printed and bound in Great Britain by
CPI Cox & Wyman Ltd, Reading, Berkshire

Contents

Many thanks to my excellent research assistant Anna Gallagher-Ross and to the Social Sciences and Research Council of Canada. I also deeply appreciate the advice of Anna Shternshis, Rona Sheramy and Jacques Kornberg. Above all, I thank my wife, Andrea Most, for her guidance, critical insights and support.

A.A.

Arthur Miller: 1915–2005

1915 17 October: Arthur Asher Miller born in New York City, the second of Isidore (Izzy) and Augusta (Gussie) Barnett Miller's three children. His brother Kermit born in 1912, sister Joan 1922.

1920–28 Attends PS 24 in Harlem, then an upper-middle-class Jewish neighbourhood, where his mother went to the same school. The family lives in an apartment overlooking Central Park on the top floor of a six-storey building at 45 West 110th Street, between Lenox and Fifth Avenues. Takes piano lessons, goes to Hebrew school and ice-skates in the park. His Barnett grandparents are nearby on West 118th Street. In summers the extended family rents a bungalow in Far Rockaway. Sees his first play in 1923, a melodrama at the Schubert Theatre.

1928 His father's successful manufacturing business in the Garment District, the Miltex Coat and Suit Company, with as many as 800 workers, begins to see hard times faced with the looming Depression. The family moves from Manhattan to rural Brooklyn, where they live at 1350 East 3rd Street, near Avenue M, in the same neighbourhood as his mother's two sisters, Annie Newman and Esther Balsam. Miller plants a pear tree in the backyard ('All I knew was cousins'). Celebrates his bar-mitzvah at the Avenue M Temple.

1930 Transfers from James Madison High School where he is reassigned to the newly built Abraham Lincoln High School on Ocean Parkway. Plays in the football team and injures his leg in a serious accident that will later excuse him from active military service. Academic record unimpressive, and he fails geometry twice.

1931 Early-morning delivery boy for a local bakery before going off to school; forced to stop when his bicycle is stolen. Works for his father during the summer vacation.

1933 Graduates from Abraham Lincoln High School and registers for night school at City College. He leaves after two weeks ('I just couldn't stay awake').

1933–34 Earns $15 a week as a clerk for Chadwick-Delamater, an automobile-parts warehouse in a run-down section of Manhattan that will later become the site for the Lincoln Center for the Performing Arts. He is the only Jewish employee, and experiences virulent anti-Semitism for the first time.

1934 Writes to the Dean of the University of Michigan to appeal against his second rejection and says he has become a 'much more serious fellow' ('I still can't believe they let me in'). Travels by bus to Ann Arbor for the autumn semester, with plans to study journalism because 'Michigan was one of the few places that took writing seriously'. Lives in a rooming house on South Division Street and joins the *Michigan Daily* as reporter and night editor; takes a non-speaking part in a student production of Shakespeare's *King Henry VIII*. Moves to an attic room at 411 North State Street and works part-time in an off-campus laboratory feeding past-prime vegetables to thousands of mice.

1936 Writes his first play *No Villain* in six days during semester break and receives a Hopwood Award in Drama for $250 using the pseudonym 'Beyoum'. Changes his major to English.

1937 Enrols in Professor Kenneth T. Rowe's playwriting class. Rewrites *No Villain* as *They Too Arise* and receives a major award of $1,250 from the Theatre Guild's Bureau of New Plays (Thomas Lanier – later Tennessee – Williams was another winner in the same competition). *They Too Arise* is produced by the B'nai Brith Hillel Players in Detroit and at the Lydia Mendelssohn Theatre in Ann Arbor. Receives a second Hopwood Award for *Honors at Dawn* when Susan Glaspell is one of the judges. Contributes to *The Gargoyle*, the student humour magazine. Drives his college friend Ralph Neaphus east to join the Abraham Lincoln Brigade in the Spanish Civil War, but decides not to go with him. Months later Neaphus, twenty-three, was dead.

1938 Composes a prison play, *The Great Disobedience*, and revises *They Too Arise* as *The Grass Still Grows*. Graduates from the University of Michigan with a BA in English. Joins the Federal Theater Project in New York to write radio plays and scripts.

1939 The Federal Theater Project is shut down by conservative forces in Congress, and Miller goes on relief. Writes *Listen My Children* and *You're Next* with his friend and fellow Michigan alumnus Norman Rosten. *William Ireland's Confession* is broadcast on the Columbia Workshop.

1940 Marries Mary Grace Slattery, his college sweetheart at the University of Michigan. They move into a small apartment at 62 Montague Street in Brooklyn Heights. Writes *The Golden Years*, a play about Montezuma, Cortez, and the European conquest and corruption of Mexico. *The Pussycat and the Plumber Who Was a Man* airs on CBS Radio. Makes a trip to North Carolina to collect dialect speech for the Folk Division of the Library of Congress.

1941–43 Works as a shipfitter's helper on the night shift at the Brooklyn Navy Yard repairing battle-scarred war vessels from the North Atlantic fleet. Finishes additional radio plays, including *The Eagle's Nest* and *The Four Freedoms*. Completes *The Half-Bridge*. The one-act *That They May Win* is produced in New York.

1944 Daughter Jane is born. Prepares Ferenc Molnar's *The Guardsman* and Jane Austen's *Pride and Prejudice* for radio adaptation, and continues his own writing for the medium. Tours army camps in preparation for the draft of a screenplay called *The Story of G.I. Joe*, based on news reports written by the popular war correspondent Ernie Pyle (withdraws from the project when his role as author is compromised). Publishes *Situation Normal …*, a book about this experience that highlights the real challenges returning soldiers encountered on re-entering civilian life. Dedicates the book to his brother, 'Lieutenant Kermit Miller, United States Infantry', a war hero. *The Man Who Had All the Luck* opens on Broadway but closes after six performances, including two previews. The play receives the Theater Guild National Award.

1945 Publishes *Focus*, a novel about anti-Semitism and moral blindness set in and around New York. His article 'Should Ezra Pound Be Shot?' appears in *New Masses*.

1946 Adapts *Three Men on a Horse* by George Abbott and John C. Holm for radio.

1947 *All My Sons* opens in New York and receives the New York Drama Critics' Circle Award, the Donaldson Award and the first Tony Award for best author. His son Robert is born. Moves with his family to a house he purchases at 31 Grace Court in Brooklyn Heights. Also buys a new car, a Studebaker, and a farmhouse in Roxbury, Connecticut. Writes the article 'Subsidized Theater' for the *New York Times*.

1948 Builds by himself a small studio on his Connecticut property where he writes *Death of a Salesman*. Edward G. Robinson and Burt Lancaster star in the film version of *All My Sons*.

1949 *Death of a Salesman*, starring Lee J. Cobb, Arthur Kennedy, Cameron Mitchell and Mildred Dunnock, opens at the Morosco Theatre in New York on 10 February. Directed by Elia Kazan with designs by Jo Mielziner, it wins the New York Drama Critics' Circle Award, the Donaldson Prize, the Antoinette Perry Award, the Theatre Club Award and the Pulitzer Prize. His essay 'Tragedy and the Common Man' is printed in the *New York Times*. Attends the pro-Soviet Cultural and Scientific Conference for World Peace at the Waldorf-Astoria Hotel to chair a panel with Clifford Odets and Dimitri Shostakovich.

1950 Adaptation of Henrik Ibsen's *An Enemy of the People* produced on Broadway starring Fredric March and Florence Henderson ('I have made no secret of my early love for Ibsen's work'). First sound recording of *Death of a Salesman*. *The Hook*, a film script about graft and corruption in the closed world of longshoremen in the Red Hook section of Brooklyn, fails to reach production after backers yield to pressure from the House Committee on Un-American Activities. *On the Waterfront*, the Budd Schulberg–Elia Kazan collaboration featuring Marlon Brando, changes the setting to Hoboken, New Jersey, but is developed from the same concept, and is released four years later.

1951 Meets Marilyn Monroe. Fredric March in the role of Willy Loman for Columbia Pictures in the first film version of *Death of a Salesman*. Joseph Buloff translates the play into Yiddish; his production runs in New York and introduces Miller's play to Buenos Aires.

1952 Drives to Salem, Massachusetts, and visits the Historical Society, where he reads documents and researches the material he will use in *The Crucible*. Breaks with Kazan over the director's cooperation with HUAC.

1953 *The Crucible* wins the Donaldson Award and the

Antoinette Perry Award when it opens in New York at the Martin Beck Theatre. Directs *All My Sons* for the Arden, Delaware, Summer Theatre.

1954 US State Department denies Miller a passport to attend the Belgian premiere of *The Crucible* in Brussels ('I wasn't embarrassed for myself; I was embarrassed for my country'). NBC broadcasts the first radio production of *Death of a Salesman*. Mingei Theater stages first Japanese translation of *Salesman* in Tokyo, where the play is received as a cautionary tale about the 'salaryman'.

1955 The one-act version of *A View from the Bridge* opens in New York on a double-bill with *A Memory of Two Mondays*. HUAC pressurises city officials to withdraw permission for Miller to make a film about juvenile delinquency set in New York.

1956 Lives in Nevada for six weeks in order to divorce Mary Slattery. Marries Marilyn Monroe. Subpoenaed to appear before HUAC on 21 June, he refuses to name names. Accepts an honorary degree as Doctor of Humane Letters from his alma mater, the University of Michigan. Jean-Paul Sartre writes screenplay for French adaptation of *The Crucible*, called *Les Sorcieres de Salem*; the film stars Yves Montand and Simone Signoret. Travels with Monroe to England, where he meets Laurence Olivier, her co-star in *The Prince and the Showgirl*. Peter Brook directs revised two-act version of *A View from the Bridge* in London at the New Watergate Theatre Club, as censors determined it could not be performed in public. 'Once Eddie had been squarely placed in his social context, among his people,' Miller noted, 'the myth-like feeling of the story emerged of itself … Red Hook is full of Greek tragedies.'

1957 Cited for contempt of Congress for refusing to co-operate with HUAC. On the steps of the United States Congress, and with Monroe on his arm, he vows to appeal against the conviction. Monroe buys all members of Congress a year's subscription to *I.F. Stone's Weekly*. First television production of *Death of a Salesman* (ITA, UK). *Arthur Miller's Collected Plays* is published, and his short story 'The Misfits' appears in *Esquire Magazine*.

1958–59 The US Court of Appeals overturns his conviction for contempt of Congress. Elected to the National Institute of Arts and Letters and receives the Gold Medal for Drama.

1961 Miller and Monroe divorce (granted in Mexico on the grounds of 'incompatibility'). *The Misfits*, a black-and-white film directed by John Huston featuring the actress in her first serious dramatic role, is released for wide distribution. Miller calls his scenario 'an eastern western' and bases the plot on his short story of the same name. Co-stars include Clark Gable, Montgomery Clift, Eli Wallach and Thelma Ritter. *The Crucible: An Opera in Four Acts* by Robert Ward and Bernard Stambler is recorded. Sidney Lumet directs a movie version of *A View from the Bridge* with Raf Vallone and Carol Lawrence. Miller's mother Augusta dies.

1962 Marries Austrian-born Inge Morath, a photographer with Magnum, the agency founded in 1947 by Henri Cartier-Bresson. Marilyn Monroe, aged thirty-six, dies. His daughter Rebecca Augusta is born in September. NBC broadcasts an adaptation of *Focus* with James Whitmore and Colleen Dewhurst.

1963 Publishes a children's book, *Jane's Blanket*. Returns to Ann Arbor to deliver annual Hopwood Awards lecture, 'On Recognition'.

1964 Visits the Mauthausen death camp with Inge Morath and covers the Nazi trials in Frankfurt, Germany, for the *New York Herald Tribune*. Reconciles with Kazan. *Incident at Vichy*, whose through-line is 'It's not your guilt I want, it's your responsibility', opens in New York, as does *After the Fall*. The former is the first of the playwright's works to be banned in the Soviet Union. The latter Miller says 'is not about Marilyn' and that she is 'hardly the play's *raison d'etre*'.

1965 Elected president of PEN, the international organisation of writers dedicated to fighting all forms of censorship. American premiere of the two-act version of *A View from the Bridge* is performed Off-Broadway. Laurence Olivier's production of *The Crucible*, starring Colin Blakely and Joyce Redman, is staged in London at the Old Vic by the National Theatre. Returns to Ann Arbor, where his daughter Jane is now a student, to participate in the first teach-in in the US concerning the Vietnam conflict.

1966 First sound recording of *A View from the Bridge*. In Rome Marcello Mastroianni and Monica Vitti play the parts of Quentin and Maggie in Franco Zeffirelli's Italian production of *After the Fall*. Miller's father Isidore dies.

1967 *I Don't Need You Any More*, a collection of short stories, is published. Sound recording of *Incident at Vichy*. Television production of *The Crucible* is broadcast on CBS. Visits Moscow and tries to persuade Soviet writers to join PEN. Playwright-in-Residence at the University of Michigan. His son Daniel is born in January.

1968 *The Price*, which the playwright called 'a quartet', 'the most specific play I've ever written', opens on Broadway. Sound recording of *After the Fall*. Attends the Democratic National Convention in Chicago as a delegate from Roxbury, Connecticut. Leads peace march against the war in South-East Asia with the Reverend Sloan Coffin, Jr, at Yale University in New Haven. *Death of a Salesman* sells its millionth copy.

1969 *In Russia*, a collaborative project with text by Miller and photography by Morath, is published. Visits Prague in a show of support for Czech writers; meets Vaclav Havel. Retires as president of PEN.

1970 Miller's works are banned in the Soviet Union, a result of his efforts to free dissident writers. *Fame* and *The Reason Why*, two one-act plays, are produced; the latter is filmed at his home in Connecticut.

1971 Television productions of *A Memory of Two Mondays* on PBS and *The Price* on NBC. Sound recording of *An Enemy of the People*. *The Portable Arthur Miller* is published.

1972 *The Creation of the World and Other Business* opens at the Schubert Theatre in New York on 30 November. Attends the Democratic National Convention in Miami as a delegate. First sound recording of *The Crucible*.

1973 PBS broadcasts Stacy Keach's television adaptation of *Incident at Vichy*, with Harris Yulin as Leduc. Champions the case of Peter Reilly, an eighteen-year-old falsely convicted of manslaughter for his mother's murder; four years later, all charges are dismissed. *After the Fall* with Faye Dunaway is televised on NBC. Teaches mini-course at the University of Michigan; students perform early drafts of scenes from *The American Clock*.

1974 *Up from Paradise*, musical version of *The Creation of the World and Other Business*, is staged at the Power Center for the Performing Arts at the University of Michigan. With music by Stanley Silverman and cover design by Al Hirschfield, Miller calls it his 'heavenly cabaret'.

1977 A second collaborative project with Inge Morath, *In the Country*, is published. Petitions the Czech government to halt arrests of dissident writers. The *Archbishop's Ceiling* opens at the Kennedy Center in Washington, DC. Miller said he wanted to dramatise 'what happens ... when people know they are ... at all times talking to Power, whether through a bug or a friend who really is an informer'.

1978 *The Theater Essays of Arthur Miller* is published. NBC broadcasts the film of *Fame* starring Richard Benjamin. Belgian National Theatre mounts the twenty-fifth anniversary production of *The Crucible*; this time Miller can attend.

1979 *Chinese Encounters*, with Inge Morath, is published. Michael Rudman directs a major revival of *Death of a Salesman* at the National Theatre in London, with Warren Mitchell as Willy Loman.

1980 *Playing for Time*, the film based on Fania Fenelon's autobiography *The Musicians of Auschwitz*, is broadcast nationally on CBS, with Vanessa Redgrave and Jane Alexander. ('I tried to treat it as a story meaningful to the survivors, by which I mean all of us. I didn't want it to be a mere horror story.') *The American Clock* has its first performance at the Spoleto Festival in South Carolina, then opens in New York with the playwright's sister Joan Copeland as Rose Baum, a role based on their mother. Miller sees his play as 'a mural', 'a mosaic', 'a story of America talking to itself ... There's never been a society that hasn't had a clock running on it, and you can't help wondering – How long?'

1981 Second volume of *Arthur Miller's Collected Plays* is published. Delivers keynote address on the fiftieth anniversary of the Hopwood Awards Program in Ann Arbor.

1982 Two one-act plays that represent 'the colors of memory', *Elegy for a Lady* and *Some Kind of Love Story*, are produced as a double-bill at the Long Wharf Theatre in Connecticut under the title *2 by A.M.*

1983 Directs *Death of a Salesman* at the People's Art Theatre in Beijing, part of a cultural exchange to mark the early stage of the opening of diplomatic relations between the United States and the People's Republic of China. Ying Ruocheng plays Willy Loman in his own Chinese translation. *I Think About You a Great Deal*, a monologue written as a tribute to Vaclav Havel, appears in *Cross Currents*, University of Michigan.

1984 *'Salesman' in Beijing* is published. The texts of *Elegy for a Lady* and *Some Kind of Love Story* are printed under a new title, *Two-Way Mirror*. Receives Kennedy Center Honors for lifetime achievement. Reworks the script of *The American Clock* for Peter Wood's London production at the National Theatre.

1985 Twenty-five million viewers see Dustin Hoffman play Willy Loman, with John Malkovich as Biff and Kate Reid as Linda in the production of *Death of a Salesman* shown on CBS. Goes to Turkey with Harold Pinter for PEN as an ambassador for freedom of speech. Serves as delegate at a meeting of Soviet and American writers in Vilnius, Lithuania, where he attacks Russian authorities for their continuing anti-Semitism and persecution of *samizdat* writers. *The Archbishop's Ceiling* is produced in the UK by the Bristol Old Vic. Completes adaptation of *Playing for Time* as a stage play.

1986 One of fifteen writers and scientists invited to meet Mikhail Gorbachev to discuss Soviet policies. The Royal Shakespeare Company uses a revised script of *The Archbishop's Ceiling* for its London production in the Barbican Pit.

1987 Miller publishes *Timebends: A Life*, his autobiography. Characterising it as 'a preemptive strike' against future chroniclers, he discusses his relationship with Marilyn Monroe in public for the first time. *Clara* and *I Can't Remember Anything* open as a double-bill at Lincoln Center in New York under the title *Danger: Memory!* Broadcasts of *The Golden Years* on BBC Radio and Jack O'Brien's television production of *All My Sons* on PBS. Michael Gambon stars as Eddie Carbone in Alan Ayckbourn's intimate production of *A View from the Bridge* at the National Theatre in London. University of East Anglia names its site for American Studies the Arthur Miller Centre.

1988 Publishes 'Waiting for the Teacher', a nineteen-stanza free-verse poem, in *Ha'aretz*, the Tel Aviv-based liberal newspaper, on the occasion of the fiftieth anniversary of the founding of the State of Israel.

1990 *Everybody Wins*, directed by Karel Reisz with Debra Winger and Nick Nolte, is released: 'Through the evolution of the story – a murder that took place before the story opens – we will be put through an exercise in experiencing reality and unreality.' Television production of *An Enemy of the People* on PBS. Josette Simon plays Maggie as a sultry jazz singer in Michael Blakemore's London revival of *After the Fall* at the National Theatre, where *The Crucible* also joins the season's repertory in Howard Davies's production starring Zoë Wannamaker and Tom Wilkinson. Updated version of *The Man Who Had All the Luck* is staged by Paul Unwin in a joint production by the Bristol Old Vic and the Young Vic in London.

1991 *The Last Yankee* premieres as a one-act play. *The Ride Down Mount Morgan*, 'a moral farce', has its world premiere in London: 'The play is really a kind of nightmare.' Television adaptation of *Clara* on the Arts & Entertainment Network. Receives Mellon Bank Award for lifetime achievement in the humanities.

1992 *Homely Girl, A Life* is published with artwork by Louise Bourgeois in a Peter Blum edition. Writes satirical op-ed piece for the *New York Times* urging an end to capital punishment in the US.

1993 Expanded version of *The Last Yankee* opens at the Manhattan Theatre Club in New York. Television version of *The American Clock* on TNT with the playwright's daughter Rebecca in the role of Edie.

1994 *Broken Glass*, a work 'full of ambiguities' that takes 'us back to the time when the social contract was being torn up', has a pre-Broadway run at the Long Wharf Theatre in Connecticut; opens at the Booth Theatre in New York on 24 April. David Thacker's London production wins the Olivier Award for Best Play.

1995 Tributes to the playwright on the occasion of his eightieth birthday are held in England and the US. Receives William Inge Festival Award for Distinguished Achievement in American Theater. *Homely Girl, A Life and Other Stories*, is published. In England the collection appears under the title *Plain Girl*. Darryl V. Jones directs a production of *A View from the Bridge* in Washington, DC, and resets the play in a community of Domincan immigrants. The Arthur Miller Society is founded by Steve Centola.

1996 Revised and expanded edition of *The Theater Essays of Arthur Miller* is published. Receives the Edward Albee Last Frontier Playwright Award. Rebecca Miller and Daniel Day-Lewis are married.

1997 *The Crucible*, produced by the playwright's son Robert A. Miller is released for wide distribution and is nominated for an Academy Award. Revised version of *The Ride Down Mount Morgan* performed at the Williamstown Playhouse in Massachusetts. BBC airs television version of *Broken Glass*, with Margot Leicester and Henry Goodman repeating their roles from the award-winning London production.

1998 *Mr Peters' Connections* opens in New York with Peter Falk. Revival of *A View from the Bridge* by the Roundabout Theatre Company wins two Tony Awards. Revised version of *The Ride Down Mount Morgan* on Broadway. Miller is named Distinguished Inaugural Senior Fellow of the American Academy in Berlin.

1999 Robert Falls's fiftieth anniversary production of *Death of a Salesman*, featuring Brian Dennehy as Willy Loman, moves from the Goodman Theater in Chicago and opens on Broadway, where it wins the Tony Award for Best Revival of a Play. Co-authors the libretto with Arnold Weinstein for William Bolcom's opera of *A View from the Bridge*, which has its world premiere at the Lyric Opera of Chicago.

2000 Patrick Stewart reprises his role as Lyman Felt in *The Ride Down Mount Morgan* on Broadway, where *The Price* is also revived (with Harris Yulin). Major eighty-fifth birthday celebrations are organised by Christopher Bigsby at the University of East Anglia and by Enoch Brater at the University of Michigan, where plans are announced to build a new theatre named in his honour; it opens officially on 29 March 2007 ('whoever thought when I was saving $500 to come to the University of Michigan that it would come to this'). 'Up to a certain point the human being is completely unpredictable. That's what keeps me going … You live long enough, you don't rust.' *Echoes Down the Corridor*, a collection of essays from 1944 to 2000, is published. Miller and Morath travel to Cuba with William and Rose Styron and meet Fidel Castro and the Colombian writer Gabriel García Márquez.

2001 Williamstown Theater Festival revives *The Man Who Had*

All the Luck. Laura Dern and William H. Macy star in a film based on the 1945 novel *Focus*. Miller is named the Jefferson Lecturer in the Humanities by NEH and receives the John H. Finley Award for Exemplary Service to New York City. His speech *On Politics and the Art of Acting* is published.

2002 Revivals in New York of *The Man Who Had All the Luck* and *The Crucible*, the latter with Liam Neeson as John Proctor. *Resurrection Blues* has its world premiere at the Guthrie Theatre in Minneapolis. Miller receives a major international award in Spain, the Premio Principe de Asturias de las Letras. Death of Inge Morath.

2003 Awarded the Jerusalem Prize. His brother Kermit Miller dies on 17 October. *The Price* is performed at the Tricycle Theatre in London.

2004 *Finishing the Picture* opens at the Goodman Theatre in Chicago. *After the Fall* revived in New York. Appears on a panel at the University of Michigan with Mark Lamos, who directs students in scenes from Miller's rarely performed plays.

2005 Miller dies of heart failure in his Connecticut home on 10 February. Public memorial service is held on 9 May at the Majestic Theatre in New York, with 1,500 in attendance. Asked what he wanted to be remembered for, the playwright said, 'A few good parts for actors.'

Plot

It is November 1938. News from Germany has reached New York of the anti-Jewish pogroms known as *Kristallnacht* or 'the Night of Broken Glass'. In Brooklyn, a Jewish-American housewife Sylvia Gellburg, who is obsessed with the newspaper reports, has become paralysed from the waist down. Doctors can find nothing wrong with her. Her condition appears to be psychosomatic. She is emotionally repressed, unhappily married to a 'self-hating Jew' and she identifies with the victims of violence.

In *Broken Glass*, Arthur Miller digs beneath the respectable veneer of family life to explore the destructive impulses that individuals turn upon themselves and the social pressures they internalise. Onstage, the neighbourhood doctor Harry Hyman leads the excavation through a series of conversations. He probes the psychological sources of both Sylvia's paralysis and her failed marriage. The domestic drama coincides with her husband Phillip's disintegration at Brooklyn Guarantee and Trust, where he heads the Mortgage Department. He makes a costly mistake, then cringing before his anti-Semitic boss, collapses of a heart attack. In the end Phillip and Sylvia are both invalids at home, where Phillip recognises the destructive power of self-hatred and suffers a second heart attack. Sylvia, in an effort to help him, manages to rise to her feet, creating an ambiguous final image of alarm and hope.

Scene One

The office and home of Dr Harry Hyman. This scene provides an exposition or background information. Phillip Gellburg waits to enquire about the condition of his wife, Sylvia. He is middle-aged, intense and dressed in black. The doctor's wife, Margaret, tells him that Hyman has been delayed because of a strike at the hospital and because his horse went lame. The image of him riding a lame horse suggests Sylvia's paralysis and foreshadows Hyman's relation to her. Margaret's lusty energy contrasts with Gellburg's limpness. She is 'fair', not Jewish, and makes the common mistake of calling him Goldberg, which reinforces his sense of being stereotyped. When the handsome, Heidelberg-educated Hyman arrives, Margaret exits. The two men trade clichés about women, and Hyman's attempt at male bonding reinforces the impression of his masculinity and Gellburg's anxiety about his own. It contributes to the stereotype of the emasculated Jewish man and associates masculinity with power. The conversation turns to Sylvia, at home in a wheelchair, as well as to news of Hitler and the smashing of Jewish stores in Berlin. Gellburg thinks that nothing can be done about anti-Semitism and that Jews bring persecution on themselves.

Hyman wants to learn more about the Gellburgs. He and other physicians have been unable to find any explanation for Sylvia's paralysis. They believe that she suffers from a 'hysterical paralysis', an affliction rooted in an unconscious trauma. Gellburg recounts the onset of the paralysis: they had been going to the movies, and suddenly her legs 'turned to butter'. Hyman probes with personal questions because 'sex could be connected'. Gellburg tensely replies that they have a healthy sex life; the physical problem started with the newspaper pictures of *Kristallnacht.* He boasts that he is the only Jew at Brooklyn Guarantee, where he heads the Mortgage Department. Finally, Hyman advises Phillip to give his wife 'a lot of loving'. After Gellburg departs, Hyman and Margaret discuss the case. They agree that Sylvia is a beautiful woman. The scene ends with him describing a fantasy with his wife on a desert island, exciting her before the blackout.

Scene Two
Next evening in the Gellburg bedroom, the 'buxom' Sylvia in a wheelchair reads a newspaper and chats to her sister

Harriet, who tidies up. Harriet expresses bewilderment at her sister's condition. They discuss Harriet's son David, who has decided not to go to college in these Depression years because it wouldn't help him to get a job. Sylvia laments the fact that she never went to college. She is curious about the world and explains why she has been riveted by the recent newspaper accounts of old Jewish men forced by Germans to clean sidewalks with toothbrushes. Harriet says it is not her business. Sylvia must stop thinking about the Germans. Sylvia returns to the paper, and Harriet leaves. Gellburg enters and surprises his wife. Following Hyman's advice and hoping to please her, he brings pickles from Flatbush Avenue, where he went to foreclose on a property. Sylvia wants to know if the tenants were nice people. Gellburg doesn't care, setting up a moral contrast between his failure to empathise and Sylvia's sympathy with strangers. Nonetheless, Sylvia feels guilty and apologises for her condition. They discuss a letter from their son Jerome, who has progressed to the rank of army captain and inspires his father with pride. Gellburg thinks it's an honour to be a West Point graduate and hopes that his son will become the first Jewish general. They bicker. Then, as the doctor ordered, Gellburg displays affection. He says he wants her to be happy. He suggests talking 'everything' out with Hyman, hinting at something traumatic in their past. There follows an elliptical conversation about trying to overcome a longstanding problem in their marriage which goes nowhere.

Scene Three

A conversation between Harriet and Dr Hyman, who is dressed in riding clothes, in his office. Harriet has come at Hyman's request to talk about her sister. She mentions that Hyman had dated her cousin twenty-five years earlier. Hyman probes to learn if Sylvia experienced any shock before her paralysis; he asks intimate questions about her marriage and her fascination with the Nazis. They discuss the oppressive character of Gellburg, who is a Republican, afflicted by Jewish self-hatred. Harriet tells a story about how Gellburg hit his wife with a steak she had overcooked, an episode that Gellburg patched up with expensive gifts. Sylvia is an innocent victim who has done nothing but love everybody. The conversation leads to speculation that, though Gellburg adores his wife, he is sexually impotent.

Scene Four
Stanton Case's office. Donning his blazer and a captain's cap, Stanton Case, President of Brooklyn Guarantee, prepares to go yachting. Gellburg comes in to discuss a property on Broadway that Case hopes to buy and renovate as an annexe for the Harvard Club. Case takes no personal interest in the obsequious Gellburg and makes a few broadly anti-Semitic remarks. Getting down to business, Gellburg explains that Case's project for the Harvard Club is dubious. Over-analysing it, Gellburg interprets recent maintenance decisions by the neighbouring retail giant, Wanamaker's Department Store, as a sign that Wanamaker's will be moving or going out of business. He concludes that the neighbourhood will depreciate in value. Case thanks him for the research, heads off to sail, and Gellburg remains with a 'self-satisfied toss of his head'.

Scene Five
Sylvia at home in bed. Hyman lets himself in, fresh from a ride on Brighton beach, suggesting interrelated themes of freedom and paralysis and analogies between the relationships of rider/horse, doctor/patient and man/woman. He sits on the bed, draws up the covers and looks appraisingly at Sylvia's legs. He compliments her strong, beautiful body. Hyman acknowledges his attraction and his own vanity. He then urges her to talk about what's bothering her and to take responsibility for herself. Sylvia wishes she could; she loves talking with the charming doctor. They recollect the days when he drove girls crazy doing acrobatics on the beach. Sylvia also expresses her

attraction to Hyman. The conversation turns to Phillip, who insisted that she should stop working when they married, though she loved her job as a bookkeeper. Hyman urges her to move; it doesn't work. They talk about his experience as a medical student in Germany and about recent pictures of *Kristallnacht* in the *New York Times*. Hyman concludes by advising Sylvia to imagine that they have made love and that she is telling him 'secret things'. He departs, and Sylvia remains, knees spread, paralysed in bed.

Scene Six

Hyman's office. As Hyman finishes with another patient, Gellburg waits and chats over cocoa with Margaret, but they irritate each other. Margaret exits. When Hyman arrives, Gellburg says that he has followed his advice about having sex with his wife. Hyman speculates that Sylvia's fear of the Nazis is a product of feeling vulnerable and unloved. Gellburg expresses his own feeling of persecution and anxiety that Sylvia is pretending paralysis to hurt him. He explains to the sexually confident Hyman that he has problems with sex. The conversation becomes more intimate. Gellburg says that he got a 'big yen' for Sylvia one night when she was sleeping and made love to her. She responded physically but the next morning claimed that she didn't remember it. He believes that his wife is trying to nullify him. According to Gellburg, she told him that he'd imagined the sex. Gellburg becomes increasingly worked up. Hyman asks abruptly if Sylvia has said anything about him. Gellburg wants to know what Hyman is up to: 'Are you a doctor or what!' He storms out. Hyman remains, guilty and alarmed. Margaret comes in and also becomes suspicious. She thinks that it might be best if Sylvia saw an actual psychiatrist. Hyman believes that Sylvia really 'knows something'. Margaret, a sensible and ironic woman, finds her husband exasperatingly self-absorbed.

Scene Seven
The office of Stanton Case. Case, in a dark mood, is angry with Gellburg for having lost him the property on Broadway. Gellburg misread the signs. Rather than going out of business, Wanamaker's had simply hired another plumber. To make matters worse, a Jewish investor has bought the property, prompting Case to suspect Gellburg of collusion because he, too, is Jewish. Gellburg insists that he is loyal to Case and begs forgiveness for his mistake. But Case remains cold, which only heightens Gellburg's anxiety.

Scene Eight
Sylvia, in a wheelchair by her bed, listens to the popular Jewish singer Eddie Cantor on the radio. Hyman arrives, and they chat about music. Hyman lifts her on to the bed, raising the sexual tension. He talks of psychoanalysis: he would need to deal with her dreams and deepest feelings, and he is not trained in psychotherapy. Nonetheless, Sylvia wants to tell him her dreams. She describes a nightmare in which a crowd of Germans are hunting for her, as in the newspaper pictures of *Kristallnacht.* She tries to run but is captured, raped and mutilated by a faceless man she identifies as her husband. Sylvia connects the dream to Gellburg's Jewish self-hatred. Hyman concludes that she is frightened of her husband; she draws the doctor to her and kisses him on the mouth. She becomes ashamed. Hyman asks if she and her husband have had sex and discovers that Gellburg lied. They haven't had sexual relations for almost twenty years, since the birth of their son. There is no clear explanation, only that Gellburg suddenly became impotent. When they were young, Sylvia's father suggested that Gellburg see a doctor, and he was so humiliated and felt so emasculated that he stopped having sex with his wife. Hyman explains that Margaret thinks there is something between himself and Sylvia, and Sylvia is pleased. She says that Phillip once hit her, drawing a connection between her husband and the Nazis. She points out that, though Hyman has said that the Germans were such nice people, they too

suddenly turned violent. She wants to know what will become of 'us'. Hyman says she's confusing two things. He's out of his depth and can't help. She takes a step off the bed in an attempt to reach him and 'the power he represents' but collapses on the floor before he can help her.

Gellburg arrives and demands to know what has happened and what Hyman is doing there. Hyman says he was worried and came to see her because Sylvia is 'desperate to be loved'. This statement is a revelation to Gellburg. After Hyman's departure, Gellburg and Sylvia discuss her conflation of attacks on Jews with their self-destructive marriage, implying the complicity of the victim. Sylvia accuses him of being a 'little liar' (like Biff to Willy in *Death of a Salesman*) for telling Hyman that they slept together, and this is followed by a moment of recognition. Sylvia exclaims: 'What I did with my life! Out of ignorance. Out of not wanting to shame you in front of other people. A whole life. Gave it away like a couple of pennies.' For Gellburg, the turning point was when she wanted to go back to work after having the baby and he insisted that she stay at home. He feels that she never forgave him for making her a housewife. But he feared that she 'didn't want him to be the man', and when she did not want more children, he dried up. He never knew why she married him because he finds his Jewish face unattractive. Gellburg insists that they have to sleep together. She says no. Weeping, he shouts that she is trying to kill him. She begins to reach out in pity before the blackout.

Scene Nine

Case's office. Gellburg, still distraught by the Wanamaker's business, has asked for a meeting to prove his dedication to the company (another scene with a parallel in *Death of a Salesman*). His whole life is there. He is more proud of his work at the company than anything except his own son. Radically insecure, he expresses his anxiety at losing Case's confidence and his sense of unfairness. Case coldly replies that he hopes his old confidence will return as time goes by, but he refuses to reassure Gellburg, who becomes hysterical, accuses Case of anti-Semitism and collapses of a heart attack.

Scene Ten

Sylvia is at home in bed, Margaret and Harriet are with her. This scene was a late addition, which Miller wrote at the request of the British director David Thacker, who wanted to see the women together before a final confrontation between the men. They discuss Gellburg's condition. Margaret and Harriet worry that Sylvia blames herself. She does, but she also acknowledges that she has always been the stronger partner, despite the pretences, and she wants to help her man. Harriet insists that Sylvia should not blame herself and that no marriage would survive if people started to say what they know. Margaret expresses the fatalistic view that a person's character is determined from infancy by genetics. The scene sets out a basic opposition between free will and determinism: each person does the best she can with the cards she's been dealt. It concludes on a note of moral ambiguity with Sylvia expressing the desire to go to her husband.

Scene Eleven

Gellburg's bedroom. Hyman examines him and urges him to go to hospital. Gellburg resists. His job, he believes, is over. He feels that his boss made a fool of him, and he is convinced that he has been unfairly treated. He also comes to the realisation that what Sylvia fears most is him. Finally, Gellburg wants to talk about being Jewish with Hyman, whom he knows is also Jewish, but someone who is not obsessed with identity. The anti-religious Hyman says that he has never pretended that he wasn't Jewish. He is a socialist. Gellberg wonders how there can be Jews if there is no God, and Hyman expresses the belief that groups will simply worship different consumer items. The scene raises the question of what it means to be a Jew and whether that identity is important. Gellburg says, 'I wouldn't know you were Jewish except for your name.' But he has also turned from his pride at being the only Jew employed at his company to the awareness that he has been exploited: 'You got some lousy rotten job to do, get Gellburg, send in the Yid.'

Building to a conclusion, Gellburg claims that 'they will never destroy us'. He wants his wife back. Hyman tells him to look in the mirror and recognise that he hates himself; that is what is scaring Sylvia to death. He concludes that Gellburg 'helped paralyse her with this "Jew, Jew, Jew" coming out of your mouth and the same time she reads it in the paper and it's coming out of the radio day and night'. Gellburg expresses a near-tragic paradox: he wants to be an Old-World Jew *and* he wants to be an assimilated American. Hyman believes that Jews don't have to be different from anybody else, and 'Everybody's persecuted'. Even Hitler has a persecution complex. There is no solution, but Gellburg should forgive Sylvia, forgive himself, forgive the Jews and forgive the goyim. Hyman leaves. Margaret pushes Sylvia in her wheelchair into Gellburg's bedroom. In their final conversation, Phillip acknowledges his fears and begs her forgiveness. On realising that he has harmed her, he seems to have another, perhaps fatal, heart attack. Sylvia struggles to break free of the wheelchair and rises to her feet. With a combination of hope and alarm she takes a faltering step towards her husband.

Commentary

The Holocaust gained enormous prominence in American culture during the 1990s, when Arthur Miller wrote his play. In 1993 the United States Memorial Holocaust Museum was dedicated on the National Mall in Washington DC, with speeches by President Bill Clinton and Nobel Peace Prize-winner Elie Wiesel, making it the dominant symbolic representation of Jewishness in America. In that same year, *Schindler's List*, which centres on the efforts of a German industrialist to save Polish Jews, became the most critically acclaimed film of Steven Spielberg's career. It won seven Oscars, including Best Picture and Best Director. On 1 March 1994, Miller's *Broken Glass*, a play that takes its title from the 1938 anti-Jewish pogrom known as *Kristallnacht*, or 'Night of Broken Glass', opened at the Long Wharf Theatre in New Haven. The play relates the failed marriage of a middle-aged Jewish couple in Brooklyn to those world-historical events. It underscores the characters' kinship to both the perpetrators and the Jewish victims of Nazi terror. It explores the theme of 'Jewish self-hatred', a term whose history dates back to the nineteenth century, and raises questions about whether identity derives from the choices people make or from something essential in their nature.

For a moralistic playwright such as Miller, anti-Semitism and the Holocaust had long been important subjects, but, unlike Clifford Odets, Saul Bellow or Philip Roth, he is not well known for making Jewish themes the focus of his major works. Critics have debated, therefore, whether Miller ought to be called a 'Jewish writer'. Christopher Bigsby, a leading scholar of his work, thinks he should. At the conclusion of *Arthur Miller: A Critical Study*, Bigsby draws a picture of Miller's Jewish origins in mystical terms: to be a Jew was to 'draw down lightning'. Jews have been the victims of numerous persecutions, and Miller made the

Holocaust his subject more than any other American dramatist. Bigsby cites references in his plays to this 'Jewish trauma' as key evidence that Miller is a Jewish writer, dating Miller to a historical moment when the Holocaust appeared to deeply inform Jewishness, at least in America. This defence of Miller's Jewish identity echoes the rhetoric of *Broken Glass*. 'I never pretended I wasn't Jewish,' says Dr Hyman, perhaps reflecting the author's point of view in the play. *Broken Glass* shows that it is impossible to locate a precise source of Jewishness and highlights the fact that many assimilationist Jews of Miller's generation erased, evaded, or worried about their Jewish origins in America. But it is less important to establish whether Miller was or wasn't a Jewish writer than to appreciate why this question came up in the first place. Written late in Miller's career, yet contemporary with the rise of 'identity politics' in America, *Broken Glass* illuminates this historical debate.

In a 1969 interview, Miller responded to a series of questions about 'Jewishness' in his work and life by saying, 'I take all this as an accusation that somehow I'm "passing" for non-Jewish. Well, I happen to have written the first book about anti-Semitism in this country in recent time. I've written numerous stories about Jews as Jews.'[1] Miller's reaction recalls a crucial theme in *Broken Glass* and in several of his other works, which represent characters that attempt to pass as non-Jews or express anxiety at being associated with Jews. The protagonist of the 1945 novel *Focus*, to which he refers, is an anti-Semitic non-Jew who is mistaken for being Jewish. The novel climaxes with a vicious attack by a racist organisation in a residential neighbourhood in Queens, New York, in which the gentile protagonist Lawrence Newman, who resembles Phillip Gellburg in *Broken Glass*, fights back-to-back with the Jewish shopkeeper Finkelstein and finally recognises a responsibility to combat a world of prejudice in which he had been complicit. It also represents a model of Jewish identity

[1] Robert A. Martin, 'Arthur Miller: Tragedy and Commitment' (1969), in Roudané, ed., *Conversations with Arthur Miller*, 184.

that is fundamentally oppositional, a struggle against stereotype.

The Holocaust – the very term Holocaust – only began to penetrate the broader American consciousness in the 1960s, after the capture and trial of the Nazi war criminal Adolf Eichmann. Although *Kristallnacht* was widely publicised and ran on the front page of the *New York Times* for nearly two weeks in 1938, the Holocaust was not central to American Jewish culture in the 1940s and 1950s. There was a reluctance to portray Jews as victims in the post-war years. Miller's plays from those decades – *All My Sons, Death of a Salesman, The Crucible, A View from the Bridge* – did not feature explicitly Jewish characters. The plays turned away from the author's origins, but they also typified the assimilationist values of that time, which are central to *Broken Glass.* In the 1930s, many Jewish immigrants' children (of which Miller was one), eager to assimilate, left behind most of the ritual practices of traditional Judaism. Eichmann's trial and execution, which attached the word 'Holocaust' to the murder of European Jews, occurred in 1962. Hannah Arendt's *Eichmann in Jerusalem: A Report on the Banality of Evil* appeared in 1963, prompting an enormous controversy because she depicted Eichmann as an ordinary bureaucrat who just followed orders and was not even particularly anti-Semitic; she noted that Jewish victims had been largely submissive; and she critiqued the role of Jewish leaders who had co-operated with the Nazis. These views led many critics to label her a self-hating Jew. Arthur Miller's first two Holocaust plays, *After the Fall* and *Incident at Vichy*, were produced the following year.

For two decades after the war, American Jews de-emphasised the idea of special Jewish victimhood. They aimed to show not simply that the Nazis were enemies of the Jews, which was common knowledge, but that they were *everyone's* enemy. The central figure of Miller's ensemble play *Incident at Vichy* is an Austrian prince, Von Berg, who, like Lawrence Newman in *Focus*, ultimately allies himself with the victims of anti-Semitism. Miller turned to the Holocaust in his 1964 plays after visiting the Mauthausen

Concentration Camp in Austria and attending the Auschwitz trials in Frankfurt with his third wife, Inge Morath. (Morath had been born in Austria and had grown up in Hitler's Germany. Her brothers had fought in the regular German army or *Werhmacht*, and her uncle had been a general.) *After the Fall* dramatises the inner life of a character named Quentin who closely resembles Miller. The drama is enacted in the shadow of a concentration camp, and when Quentin's thoughts turn to the Jewish cemetery there, he realises that he is less moved by thoughts of the murdered Jews than is his German lover, Holga. The play suggests that humanity in general was guilty of the Holocaust, not just the Germans. In 1994, approaching the fiftieth anniversary of the liberation of the concentration camps, the Holocaust also spoke to other, more recent genocides, a connection Miller himself was quick to draw: 'Look at the Second World War. Look at Vietnam, Korea, Rwanda, the Balkans . . . We're savages.'[1] Miller's pessimistic message reflects the universalising outlook that makes everyone a victim (and a victimiser). Far from suggesting a particularly Jewish tragedy, Miller taps into the post-war view that we are basically all the same and that anti-Semitism is only one form of hatred, essentially no different from others.

Context

Kristallnacht

Within twenty-four hours on 9–10 November 1938, the Nazi Reich unleashed a massive wave of violence against the Jews of Germany. The National Socialists (Nazis) had taken power in Germany in 1933 with an explicitly anti-Semitic agenda under the leadership of Adolf Hitler. Between 1935 and 1938, the situation of Jews in Germany grew increasingly desperate. In 1935, the Nuremberg Laws classified who was Jewish and made it easier to pass further

[1] Interview with Michael March. 29 October 2001. http://www.guardian.co.uk/books/2001/oct/29/stage.arthurmiller.

legislation restricting human rights for its Jewish citizens. The Nuremberg Laws deprived assimilated Jews of German citizenship and prohibited marriage between Jews and other Germans. They restricted the professions Jews could enter and deprived them of numerous other civil and political rights. In the United States, the Neutrality Acts of 1935 and 1937 passed by an isolationist Congress prevented the administration of President Franklin Delano Roosevelt from intervening in conflicts overseas. In *Broken Glass*, Sylvia's paralysis evokes America's neutrality as the Nazis annexed Austria and Czechoslovakia, perpetrated *Kristallnacht* and invaded Poland in 1939, precipitating the Second World War. Roosevelt, who became a great wartime president, was confined to a wheelchair, and there is a brief discussion in the play about whether Sylvia's paralysis was caused by polio (it wasn't), which was the source of FDR's condition. In this way, Sylvia too becomes a figure for America. Miller's play raises questions about neutrality and isolationism not only in the 1930s but also in the 1990s, when it was written, and America again debated intervention in foreign conflicts from Iraq to Yugoslavia to Rwanda.

On 11 March 1938, the Austrian Nazi party executed a bloodless coup d'état. On 12 March, the German army marched into Austria in what was known as the Anschluss. It was part of Hitler's aim to restore a German-speaking empire in lands that had been lost to Germany in the First World War. There was virtually no opposition from France and Great Britain, which were practising a policy known as appeasement. Eager to avoid war with Germany, they sought to settle matters by compromise and negotiation rather than military confrontation. Five weeks before *Kristallnacht* they negotiated an agreement for Germany to annex the Sudetenland (the western regions of Czechoslovakia inhabited at that time mostly by ethnic Germans), which the British Prime Minister, Neville Chamberlain, claimed would bring 'peace in our time'. The Allies' policy is now associated with weakness and cowardice. In *Broken Glass*, the inability to walk, let alone rise up and fight, hints at this failure to stand up to Nazi aggression. The German-educated Hyman says, 'I simply can't imagine those people marching into Austria, and now they say Czechoslovakia's next, and Poland.' *Kristallnacht* marked the culmination of a year in which Hitler dramatically expanded German power in Europe. It was a milestone on the road to the Second World War. The historian Martin Gilbert notes that 'no other event in the history of the fate of German Jews between 1933 and 1945 was so widely covered by newspapers while it was taking place.'[1] It changed the way Nazism was perceived.

The foreground of *Kristallnacht* began in October 1938, when Hitler ordered more than 12,000 Polish-born Jews to be expelled from Germany. Most lost everything they had earned in their decades of working and living in Germany. They were taken at gunpoint by the Gestapo to the nearest railway stations and sent to the Polish border, where the vast majority were denied entry and left in limbo. The daughter of one expelled family sent a desperate postcard to her seventeen-year-old brother Herzschel Grynszpan, who was living in Paris. The next morning Grynszpan read a vivid description of the plight of these Polish Jews in a Yiddish-language newspaper. On Sunday he bought a pistol. Monday morning he went to the German Embassy and shot the Third Secretary Ernst vom Rath. In Germany, the newspapers of 8 November denounced all Jewish people as murderers. Numerous punitive measures were put in place. Jewish periodicals were shut down. Jewish children could no longer attend 'Aryan' elementary schools and a number of demonstrations against Jews erupted throughout Germany, including vandalism of Jewish shops and synagogues.

On the evening of 9 November, news reached Berlin that vom Rath had died. German radio stations observed two minutes of silence, and crowds began to converge in thoroughfares where Jews were gathered, such as the French tourist office in Berlin, where Jews waited to get the travel details they needed in order to emigrate. The Nazi

[1] Martin Gilbert, *Kristallnacht* (London: Harper Press, 2006), 16.

command, including Hitler and his Minister of Propaganda, Josef Goebbels, encouraged anti-Jewish demonstrations and withdrew the police, unleashing an orgy of violence against Jewish men, women and children in thousands of cities, towns and villages throughout Germany and Austria. Squads of young men roamed through Berlin's major shopping districts, breaking shop windows, looting and tossing merchandise into the streets. Thousands of storefronts were smashed, shops and houses looted, synagogues burned and holy objects desecrated. Jews, who were minding their own business, were set upon in the streets. They were chased, beaten and humiliated. Ninety-one Jews were killed. More than 30,000 Jewish men were arrested and sent to concentration camps, where they were tortured and where thousands died. In Vienna, twenty-two Jews were reported to have committed suicide. In Frankfurt, storm-troopers known as Brownshirts burned all of the synagogues, destroyed windows, goods and equipment in every Jewish shop and office, and arrested 2,000 Jews, including all rabbis, religious leaders and teachers. News spread of other indignities. In one town a Romanian Jew was forced to crawl for two and a half miles, beaten continually by hooligans. In *Broken Glass*, Sylvia reads reports of jeering crowds forcing old men with beards to crawl and scrub the pavements with toothbrushes.

Restricted to her bed or wheelchair, Sylvia's position in her Brooklyn apartment is meant to be analogous to that of incarcerated European Jews, yet it also suggests the fine aspects of her identification with those degraded and non-particularised 'others'. Rather than leading to political engagement, her identification and paralysis literalise the disempowerment she has experienced in her marriage to the tyrannical Phillip. She gave up the freedoms she had enjoyed, presumptive rights to an education and to work, when she entered into marriage, not unlike the European Jews whose relationship to the dominant German culture was often depicted as feminised. German Jews, enfranchised only in the late nineteenth century, were stripped of civil rights by the Nuremberg Laws. *Kristallnacht* proved that not only the riff-raff but also the educated German middle class that Hyman fondly remembers in the play were complicit in brutalising their Jewish fellow citizens.

Historians have debated the American response to *Kristallnacht.* Despite alarming reports in the press from the time of the German invasion of Austria in March to the pogroms in November, American anti-immigration and refugee attitudes did not substantially relax or lead to a new policy. Although the United States was officially neutral, many Americans called for the government to do something, while nativists refused to open doors to refugees and isolationists insisted that the US keep out of European conflicts. Some of this debate is reflected in *Broken Glass.* Gellburg expresses a bias against German Jews who 'won't take an ordinary good job' and 'can't even speak English'. Sylvia exclaims, '*This is an emergency!* They are beating up little children! What if they kill those children! Where is Roosevelt! Where is England! You've got to do something before they murder us all!' Negative sentiments towards Germany intensified, but American attitudes against refugees stiffened.[1] President Roosevelt denounced the attacks. He recalled the American ambassador to Berlin as a gesture of protest against the Nazi-sponsored pogrom and announced that he would extend visitors' permits for the 12,000–15,000 German refugees already in America, but other policy initiatives died in the Committee on Immigration and Naturalization in the House of Representatives. In February 1939, public opinion against admitting Jewish refugees led Congress to reject the Wagner–Rogers Bill, which would have admitted 20,000 Jewish children. American Jewish organisations, wary of inciting anti-Semitism at home, did not protest. Later in 1939 the German cruise ship *St Louis* carrying approximately 900 Jewish refugees was turned away from American shores and sent back to Europe.

The American press gave the events of November 1938

[1] Deborah E. Lipstadt, *Beyond Belief: the American Press and the Coming of the Holocaust, 1933–1945* (New York: Free Press, 1986), 98.

massive coverage. Nearly every important newspaper in the country, from the *Washington Post* to the *Chicago Tribune* to the *San Francisco Chronicle*, covered the story and expressed outrage at the 'Nazi terror'. *Kristallnacht* was on the front page of the *New York Times* for more than a week. On 10 November, it ran a front-page story, 'Berlin Raids Reply to Death of Envoy: Nazis Loot Jews' Shops, Burn City's Biggest Synagogue to Avenge Paris Embassy Aide.' The next day's headlines reported that all of Vienna's twenty-one synagogues had been attacked and Jews beaten under the direction of storm-troopers and Nazi party members in uniform. Thousands of Jews were arrested, and the *New York Times* speculated on 11 November, in 'Bands Rove City', that they were being held as hostage for the 'good behavior of Jewry outside Germany'. In almost every town and city in Hitler's Reich the looting and destruction continued. On 13 November, the *New York Times* reported that Germany had issued a new series of decrees calling for the complete 'liquidation of the Jews'. These newspaper reports become Sylvia's obsession in *Broken Glass* and reflect the other characters' lack of interest in current events or their active state of denial. The wartime death of European Jews, though the numbers would soon escalate, was never again reported so prominently in the American media. Miller, who was working in the Brooklyn Navy Yard, noted 'the near absence among men I worked with [in 1942] . . . of any comprehension of what Nazism meant – we were fighting Germany essentially because she had allied herself with the Japanese who had attacked us at Pearl Harbor'[1] – not, in other words, because of the Holocaust.

Jews in America

American Jewry has never been a monolithic group. *Broken Glass* represents a microcosm of Jewish society in the late 1930s that explicitly resists homogeneity. At the end of the

[1] Quoted in Paul Fussell, *Wartime* (New York: Oxford University Press, 1990), p. 138.

play, Gellburg tells Hyman, 'I wouldn't know you were Jewish except for your name.' Even the name is not a give-away. Hyman's wife Margaret has taken his last name but is not Jewish. Hyman points out that there are Chinese Jews, which prompts Gellburg to wonder what he has been looking for in the mirror over the years, as he tried to discover what made his features Jewish. As Sylvia says, 'A Jew can have a Jewish face.' But what is a Jewish face? Hyman, who is also a Jew, does not have one. For Gellburg, being a Jew is at least as much a performance as it is rooted in anything in his nature; it is, as he says, 'a full-time job'.

Gellburg's resistance to the stereotypical model of the American Jew is indicated by the repeated mistake that Margaret Hyman makes at the beginning of the play in calling him Goldberg. 'It's Gellburg, not Goldberg,' he says. To which she replies after he painstakingly spells his name, 'It does sound like Goldberg.' *The Goldbergs* was a popular comedy-drama created by actor-writer Gertrude Berg and broadcast from 1929 to 1946 on American radio. The show featured both the Jewish ethnicity of the Goldbergs and the story of their assimilation to American life. On several occasions Berg, who wrote all the episodes until the late thirties, incorporated serious historical issues. An episode on 3 April 1939 addressed *Kristallnacht* when the family's Passover Seder was interrupted by a rock thrown through the window. Later episodes referred to friends or family members trying to escape Eastern Europe, though most avoided direct discussion of politics and focused on the family. A few other details of *The Goldbergs* illuminate aspects of *Broken Glass.* The television version, which ran on CBS from 1949 to 1951, co-starred Philip Loeb as Jake Goldberg. Loeb, who shares his first name with Miller's character Phillip Gellburg (the original title for *Broken Glass* was *Gellburg*), was blacklisted during the McCarthy period when many members of the entertainment industry were accused – often unfairly – of Communist sympathies, and NBC subsequently convinced Berg to let him go in 1950.

With the exception of Margaret Hyman and Gellburg's boss, Stanton Case, all of the characters in *Broken Glass* are

Jewish. Gellburg and Hyman in particular represent contradictions of twentieth-century American Jewish experience. There does not seem to be anything essentially Jewish about Hyman. He doesn't think about being Jewish or act in a noticeably Jewish way. Aside from his name, the one sign of Hyman's Jewishness is a single spoken line of Yiddish, but it is couched in both humanist terms and an American idiom: 'I think you get further faster, sometimes, with a little common sense and some plain human sympathy. Can we talk turkey? *Tuchas offen tisch*, you know any Yiddish?' Hyman, like Arthur Miller, may know some idiomatic Yiddish, but he prefers to 'talk turkey', common sense and 'human sympathy' instead of using any tribal affiliation. Gellburg obsessively resists Jewish identification. Ironically, this resistance makes him the most ethnically marked character in the play. Although he does understand Yiddish, his allegiance is less to 'human sympathy' than it is to America. He has married a Jewish woman, Sylvia, but he hopes that his son Jerome, a West Point graduate and captain in the Army, will become the first Jewish general. (In real life, the most famous Jewish man in the military at that time was Hyman Rickover, who became a four-star Admiral and 'Father of the Nuclear Navy'.) Jerome's accomplishments and the dreams of his father seem grafted from those of Miller, who recalls in *Timebends* that as a child he had been 'programmed to choose something other than pride in my origins' (24). His dreams too had been military rather than spiritual: 'If ever any Jews should have melted into the proverbial pot, it was our family in the twenties; indeed I would soon be dreaming of entering West Point, and in my most private reveries I was no sallow Talmud reader' but a hero of 'athletic verve and military courage' (62). Like Miller, Hyman has married a non-Jew, known often disparagingly in Yiddish as a 'shiksa', and does not make a Jewish home. He has what Gellburg considers a non-Jewish hobby: he rides horses. He is a secularist and claims that he is not afraid of anyone, but when Gellburg wonders if he married a non-Jew so that he wouldn't seem Jewish, Hyman replies 'coldly': 'I never pretended I wasn't

Jewish.' In 1939, Miller himself was married to a 'shiksa' (none of his three wives were Jewish, though his second wife, Marilyn Monroe, was a convert). In *Timebends*, he comments, 'There was a deep shadow then over intermarriage between Jews and gentiles' (70). Intermarriage rates were low in the 1930s, partly because young Jews and Christians did not interact in social situations enough to fall in love. Miller's other best friends in college at the University of Michigan, Norman Rosten and Hedda Rowinski, were Jews (and later married each other). In marrying a non-Jew, Miller made a choice about which *Broken Glass* expresses sensitivity when Dr Hyman defends his decision to marry Margaret. To Miller, religion in the time of the Depression seemed absurdly irrelevant. Hyman expresses the same view.

However, Gellburg's anxieties about being Jewish are by no means unfounded. The interwar years were characterised by an upsurge of nativism, xenophobia, racism and anti-Semitism, which included growing prejudice even against Jews whose families had been in the country for generations. The Red Scare of 1919–20, which targeted suspected communists, was one source of anti-Jewish feeling, and the Great Depression made social tensions worse. Polls indicate that anti-Semitism was high in the 1930s; as late as 1940 a majority of Americans found that Jews' most objectionable quality was their supposed 'unscrupulousness'. From the 1920s to the 1930s universities from Harvard and Yale to Illinois and Kansas restricted the number of Jewish students by quotas and other means. Hotels, clubs, fraternities and resorts barred Jews, as Miller shows in his novel *Focus*. Many companies would not hire Jewish employees. Hyman interned at Mount Sinai Hospital, which was founded to address the needs of New York's Jewish immigrants, and Gellburg is proud of being the sole Jewish employee of Brooklyn Guarantee. In the 1930s 'restrictive covenants' excluded Jews from buying real estate in exclusive neighbourhoods. Physical violence against Jews also increased during the 1920s with attacks by the Ku Klux Klan and, in the 1930s, by German-Americans sympathetic to Hitler. Father Charles Coughlin, a pro-Nazi, rabid isolationist and opponent of Roosevelt's New Deal policies, had a radio programme which reached forty million listeners in the 1930s, spewing anti-Semitic vitriol. His Social Justice movement had mass appeal. For the most part, American Jews in the 1930s stayed among their own kind. That was Miller's experience growing up in Manhattan and Brooklyn, and it is the experience of the small group of characters in *Broken Glass*, except for Gellburg's interaction with Stanton Case, whom he sees only at work. American Jews of the 1930s did not need to be religious to know that they were Jews. It was not synagogue attendance, but Jewish food in the kitchen (Miller's mother made brisket, gefilte fish and *tsimmes*), Yiddish inflections in everyday conversation and close proximity to other Jews that gave a Jewish feel to a neighbourhood.

Ethnic identity often expressed itself though political affiliation. Hyman believes not in God or even religion, but, like Miller himself at the time in which the play is set, in socialism. Gellburg, trying hard to be un-Jewish, is a pro-capitalist Republican. Most American Jews fell between the two and were strong supporters of Roosevelt's New Deal. In Miller's 1992 novella *Plain Girl*, which shares many themes with *Broken Glass*, the protagonist tells her brother, 'You must be the last Republican Jew in New York.' In 1936, 85 per cent of American Jews voted against the Republicans and for Democratic President Roosevelt. By 1940 it was 90 per cent. There is some merit to the accusation that American Jews were so enamoured of the Roosevelt administration that they failed to push harder for rescue operations after *Kristallnacht*. But Jews hardly formed a single political block on this issue, and their responses to the Holocaust ranged widely, as in the play, from psychic breakdown to relative indifference. Sylvia paradoxically feels that something must be done for the victims of *Kristallnacht* and becomes paralysed, while Gellburg worries that too much sympathy for the victims might excite anti-Semitism in America.

Broken Glass also suggests a trace of Jewish divisions

transplanted from the Old World to the New between more affluent, assimilated Jews of German origin and those from Eastern Europe. It represents American prejudices against recent immigrants. Miller's mother Gussie frequently voiced these prejudices. His father Isidore emigrated from Poland at the age of six, while Gussie had been born in New York, and she never let him forget it. She looked down on her husband's lack of education and, though she enjoyed the luxuries of their haute-bourgeois life before the stock-market crash of 1929, she often gave voice to anti-Semitic rhetoric about 'Jews who care for nothing but business'. Although her background was not far removed from that of the recent immigrants, she felt superior for being a native-born American and not a 'greenhorn' like those who grew up on Manhattan's Lower East Side. In the 1920s, in their posh apartment the Millers lived among the more cultured and affluent German Jews. Dr Hyman, who stays in Brooklyn because of his political ideals, would have been accepted in that company. On the other hand, orthodox Jews, though also divided into feuding camps, seem to Gellburg to be the true Jews: 'there are some days I feel like going and sitting in the Schul [synagogue] with the old men and pulling the *tallis* [prayer shawl] over my head and be a full-time Jew the rest of my life. [...] And other times . . . yes, I could almost kill them.' It is shocking to hear this rhetoric coming from a Jewish character in 1938. Moreover, Gellburg here seems to assume what many orthodox Jews would, that Reform or secularised Jews were not real Jews at all.

The play never represents a coherent sense of what constitutes Jewish identity, in part because there is no single way to answer this question. But its failure to resonate with American audiences in the 1990s stems in part from the fact that, while addressing contemporary concerns with identity and the Holocaust, it draws its rhetoric and its deepest preoccupations, like much of Miller's work, from the 1930s. There is no trace of the ethnic pride that characterised the most successful Jewish American playwright of the 1990s, Tony Kushner, whose exuberant two-part 'fantasia' *Angels in*

America and whose adaptation of S. Anski's Yiddish play *A Dybbuk* also explicitly draw on Holocaust themes. But Kushner's work was only part of a broader theatrical investment in expressing, rather than repressing, the particularised 'traumas' that set distinctive groups of Americans apart from each other, often as defined victim communities. Important playwrights of this period include María Irene Fornés, August Wilson, David Henry Hwang, Luis Valdez and Susan-Lori Parks. Miller's 1994 play is informed by the revival of ethnic identity in American culture, yet its characters aspire to a national or humanistic rather than an ethnic source of identity. Gellburg's self-hatred and Hyman's idealism date from a more earnest time, signified by Gellburg's heart, which attacks him not once but twice. Hyman, like Miller, may not pretend not to be Jewish, but he doesn't feel much like talking about it either. His assertion that Gellburg will find the root of the problem if he looks at himself in the mirror and that *he* paralysed his wife with 'Jew, Jew, Jew' coming out of his mouth, sounds not only troublingly anti-Semitic and counter to the ethos of American drama in the 1990s, but also, and even more problematic, in aligning Gellburg with the Nazis, it suggests that the Jews themselves may be complicit in their own destruction.

Broken Glass reflects the heavy sense of culpability from the 1970s through the 1990s for American failures to rescue European Jews from the Holocaust. The figure of the paralysed American Jew in *Broken Glass* and the rhetoric of responsibility taps into the historical soul-searching of more recent Holocaust studies, as illustrated by books with titles such as *The Abandonment of the Jews*, *The Failure to Rescue*, *While Six Million Died*, *No Haven for the Oppressed* and *The Jews Were Expendable*. When the paralysed Sylvia becomes transfixed by the pictures of humiliated German Jews in the newspapers, her sister says, 'What business of it is yours?' In the 1990s many believed that not only Americans but also American Jews in particular had a lot to atone for. In 1993, the chairman of the Holocaust Museum's education committee told the press that those who did nothing were 'just as guilty' as those who performed the killing.[1] Few people spoke this way in the thirties, and most Americans felt proud of the sacrifices they made to defeat Hitler. This morality-play version of history, to which Miller has been attracted in other works, such as *Incident at Vichy*, has been much disputed by historians. Invoking *Kristallnacht* and the Holocaust as the prime indicators that we are all victims, *Broken Glass* enters troubling moral waters. It exposes cowardice, timidity and self-hatred, but the characters find it difficult, if not impossible, to converse in a moderate, balanced or nuanced way. When Gellburg says, 'I wish we could talk about the Jews', Hyman becomes evasive. *Kristallnacht* heralded the Holocaust to come, but it remains unclear what, if anything, American Jews could have done to save lives in Europe. Sylvia's plight suggests a more ambiguous moral. Paralysed as she obsesses over images of old men on the pavements of Berlin, she rises to her feet in the end to reach not a distant and abstract image of a Jew but her unconscious husband, collapsed in front of her. Like most people, she becomes able to take action when presented with an immediate personal situation in which she feels that she can make a difference.

In its diverse characters, *Broken Glass* represents competing attitudes towards assimilation and anti-Semitism, yet by 1994 most American Jews were assimilated, and anti-Semitism in the United States, though still present, was on the decline. For an author feeling the sting of accusations that he had turned his back on his people, the Holocaust was the obvious theme to address feelings of guilt on both a personal and a more broadly historical level. As the stricken husband says at the end of the play, 'Why we're different I will never understand.' Gellburg's overpowering sense of his own difference makes him almost a tragic figure, though not a hero. However misguided his aspirations, he represents the failure of an individual to liberate himself from the crushing social codes that he has internalised. Although his

[1] Helen Fagin on *ABC World News Tonight*, 21 April 1993; Peter Novick, *The Holocaust in American Life* (New York: Mariner Books, 2000), 48.

collapse at the end of the play is not necessarily fatal, the final tableau implies that his destruction is necessary for Sylvia to find new life.

The Great Depression

Arthur Miller was born into an upper-middle-class family. His father at one time employed 800 people in his women's coat company, and the family lived in a Manhattan apartment overlooking Central Park North. But Isidore Miller had borrowed to invest in the stock market, where people were making much more money in the 1920s. On Black Thursday, 24 October 1929, the US Stock Market collapsed and the Great Depression began. It was an economic crisis that affected nearly every country in the world. Although Isidore's business did not fail, he lost all of his savings and investments in stocks. Soon the family lost the trappings of American success: the car and chauffeur, the maid, the apartment in Manhattan. They moved to a house in Brooklyn, and the fourteen-year-old Arthur Miller had to share a bedroom with his grandfather.

Many of Miller's plays represent a weak or defeated father and a sympathetic mother, an Oedipal drama that Miller drew partly from his own experience. He was his mother's favourite, and he was deeply affected by his father's failures both in business and as a figure of authority at home. His mother verbally abused his father for his shortcomings, and Miller tended to agree with her, feeling that his father had failed the family. At the same time, he expressed contradictory emotions, and he blamed the American economic system. *Broken Glass* follows this Oedipal pattern in its sympathetic portrayal of the beautiful Sylvia, who resents giving up her education and work before her marriage, and its brutal presentation of the floundering Phillip, the weak and exhausted Jew, though Phillip seems a solid breadwinner until shortly before the end of the play. This dynamic not only characterised the Miller household but also reflected the aftermath of the Wall Street Crash, which Miller always regarded as a formative influence on his life.

In 1934, Miller moved from Brooklyn to the University of Michigan, feeling guilty about leaving his brother Kermit to prop up the family while he, the inferior student, went off to college. But the activist environment of Michigan was the making of him. He wrote for the *Michigan Daily*; he became engaged in left-wing political activities. Like Dr Hyman, he met his first wife, a non-Jew, as a student, and she became his assistant, typing his manuscripts, and sharing his socialist political convictions. It is unclear whether he joined the Communist Party, but during the 1930s he was an active sympathiser. While he was at college, his father gave up on his company and joined the ranks of the unemployed and assumed the look of defeat. Collapse of the market led to collapse of families, and the plays Miller wrote in college reflected this awareness. His 1936 play *They Too Arise* is about a Jewish family struggling to overcome a looming business failure. In addition to winning a college writing prize, the play was staged in Ann Arbor and Detroit.

To many people during the Depression, it seemed that there was a sudden inexplicable loss of coherence. *Broken Glass* represents a world falling apart, a society of scarcity, and it touches on the characters' deepest anxieties. Hyman is late for an appointment at the beginning of the play not only because his horse goes lame but also because the new union pulled a strike at the hospital. Sylvia's inexplicable paralysis evokes this historical sense of confusion and collapse. But the opening lines also shed light on the bewildering demise of Gellburg, who tries (too hard) to do everything right. He represents particular social anxieties. Gellburg is a social climber, uncertainly allied with the establishment moneyed class. He manages to hold on to a handsome pay cheque as long as he works for Stanton Case. His sister-in-law Harriet says, 'There's no Depression for Phillip.' But, in fact, Gellburg is a lightning rod of the Depression; he expresses the anti-refugee sentiment of the Republican Party, of Congress and of the vast majority of the American public. He acknowledges that his line of work has given him direct knowledge of the economic and social impact of the Depression; he personally oversaw the foreclosures 'left and right' in the severe downturns of 1932 and 1936. With high unemployment, most people, like Gellburg, were in favour of reducing quotas for new immigrants, and legislation to that effect was introduced repeatedly in the US House of Representatives. Furthermore, 1937–8 coincided with the worst phase of the 'Roosevelt Recession', when unemployment began to rise again, and Democrats suffered losses in the 1938 Congressional elections. Thus, Gellburg resents immigrants competing for American jobs when the latest official figure is twelve million unemployed, and he resents the Roosevelt administration's investment in welfare, the Works Progress Administration, designed to put people back to work at government expense, also reflecting political debates about the welfare reform of the 1990s. Hyman remarks, 'You're very unusual . . . you almost sound like a Republican.' And Gellburg replies, 'Why? – The Torah says a Jew has to be a Democrat?' Self-conscious about his difference, Gellburg evinces his own insecurity.

Miller came of age during the 1930s, and *Broken Glass* harks back to some elements of the agitprop (agitation and propaganda) theatre that influenced him then, specifically in the urgency of its central message that people should not only protest but do something about injustice. He adopted large social themes in plays throughout his career. In 1938 Miller returned to New York, where he managed briefly to gain the support of the WPA's Federal Theatre and Writers Project, at $22.77 per week. As the reverberations of *Kristallnacht* were felt in late 1938, Miller exulted that he had managed to secure a studio apartment with a desk and a rug. However, the Federal Theatre Project was targeted by a Congressional committee that aimed to ferret out every 'subversive' group in the country. The committee alleged that the Federal Theatre Project was producing communist propaganda, and discontinued its funding in 1939. 'The Depression taught us that we were all equally victims,' Miller has said.

> Suddenly we were all the victims of something unseen and unknowable, and none of us was any worse than the other guy [...] we were no longer individuals. And then came along psychology to tell us that we were again the victim of drives that we weren't even conscious of, so that the idea of man being willfully good or willfully bad evaporated. We are nothing but what we were born and what we were taught to be up to the age of six. And we are essentially irresponsible. I think that's the situation we're in now.[1]

These themes – universal victimisation, loss of individuality, Freudian psychology, personal responsibility and in-born guilt – inform his entire body of work, and they are central to *Broken Glass*. Although the drama taps into the 1990s obsession with identity, it retains traces of the concerns that made Miller's early plays so resonant: the instability of class, the harm of buying into conventional wisdom and the logic of capitalism, and the extension of the macroeconomic effects of the Great Depression to the microcosm of an individual family.

Holocaust plays

The problem of representing the unrepresentable is the central moral and aesthetic issue of Holocaust dramas. Should a writer attempt to bear witness by staging atrocity with scrupulous realism, or obliquely render horrors whose enormity defies conventional representation? Holocaust drama has been characterised by the tension between maintaining a reverent silence about atrocities too horrible to depict on stage and giving voice to the events that must never be forgotten. Gene A. Plunka provides a comprehensive list of representative Holocaust dramas and their respective dramatic forms: 'realism (Arthur Miller's *Incident at Vichy*), epic theatre (Tony Kushner's *A Bright Room Called Day*), surrealism (George Tabori's *The Cannibals*), black comedy (Peter Barnes's *Laughter!*), verse drama (Nelly Sach's

[1] Quoted in Philip Gelb, 'Morality and Modern Drama' (1958), in Roudané, ed., *Conversations with Arthur Miller*, 49.

Eli), melodrama (Frances Goodrich and Albert Hackett's *The Diary of Anne Frank*), classical tragedy (Rolf Hochhuth's *The Deputy*) and documentary theatre (Peter Weiss's *The Investigation*)' (Plunka, 17–18).

The most famous Holocaust drama in America remains the Pulitzer Prize-winning adaptation of *The Diary of Anne Frank* by Albert Hackett and Francis Goodrich. But there were relatively few 'Holocaust plays' in America during the immediate post-war years, when few could see the value of dramatising such a horrifying subject. Most American Jews at that time wanted to be treated like other Americans, not singled out as a suffering minority. Jews were more interested in integrating into American society than in standing out. The play version of *The Diary of Anne Frank* was no exception to the tendency to treat the Holocaust not as a catastrophe particular to the Jews but as an ordeal visited upon all of humanity by the Nazis. The 1955 Broadway play, which also won the Tony for Best Play and the New York Drama Critics' Circle Award, was a box-office smash and was made into a movie four years later. By the 1990s, when attitudes about the Holocaust had changed and Miller wrote *Broken Glass*, *Anne Frank* was often condemned for its universalistic and optimistic moral, that 'in spite of everything . . . people are really good at heart'. Critics faulted the adapters for removing Anne's Jewishness from the play. But, like many Americans of her generation, the Dutch Anne Frank was an assimilated girl who expressed little awareness of specifically Jewish values or rituals.

Themes of guilt and responsibility are central to the German Protestant playwright Rolf Hochhuth's play *Der Stellvertreter* (*The Deputy*), which opened in 1964 on Broadway in its English translation. The play led to violent demonstrations, mostly between Protestants and Catholics, in Europe. Its subject was the failure of Pope Pius XII to denounce the Holocaust during the war. In the United States, Jewish leaders, who wanted good relations with Christians, were lobbied heavily by Catholics to denounce the play and to put pressure on the director and producer to cancel the production. For the most part the leaders of the

Anti-Defamation League and the American Jewish Committee complied, but the play went on anyway, though it was not a success and plans for a national tour were cancelled. Nonetheless, the dispute over this play was another milestone in the evolving discourse of the Holocaust in America. Like Miller, Hochhuth emphasises the importance of the individual assuming responsibility.

Following the immediate post-war era, there was a revival or 'renaissance' in Holocaust drama, from the seventies to the nineties, which included Miller's film, later adapted as a play, *Playing for Time* (1980) and *Broken Glass* (1994). *Playing for Time* is based on the autobiography of Fania Fenelon, a Jewish musician who was imprisoned in Auschwitz. The Israeli playwright Joshua Sobol's *Ghetto* (1984) draws on similar themes, as well as first-hand accounts and archival documents. Based on a theatre that was established in the famous Jewish ghetto in Vilna, Lithuania, *Ghetto* advocates the importance of preserving Jewish culture. By the late nineties, an estimated 150 to 250 Holocaust dramas had been produced in the US, Europe and Israel. Premiering two years after *Broken Glass*, Harold Pinter's play *Ashes to Ashes* (1996) also examines the relationship of the personal to the political. Rebecca and Devlin, like Sylvia and Phillip, undergo a wrenching form of self-analysis, which associates the husband's authoritarian personality with the Nazi regime. Devlin, Rebecca's husband (or lover), is also her therapist and potentially her murderer, while she, like Sylvia, feels a deep connection to the persecuted Jews. Miller's dramas, including *Incident at Vichy* and *After the Fall*, are frequently cited as significant contributions to Holocaust drama from the 1960s to the 1990s.

Themes

Guilt

Guilt – one of the dominant subjects of Miller's entire body of work – is central to *Broken Glass*. Each of the three central characters expresses a sense of guilt at some point in the play: Hyman for marital infidelities and for improper advances to his female patient, Gellburg for infractions at work and at home, and Sylvia for imposing her infirmity on others. Often the guilt has no clear source, and characters beg each other for forgiveness, while others reply that there is nothing to forgive. The play represents both a sense of broken faith with ethnic affiliations – Jews who turn their backs on other Jews or on aspects of themselves – and a broader notion of global culpability in the abandonment of the Nazi victims described in the newspapers. In *Broken Glass* and elsewhere, Miller implies that everyone is complicit in Nazi war crimes and the slaughter of innocents. He follows the line of a revisionist school in Holocaust history, popular in the late 1960s, which argues that Western democracies, the Pope, neutral countries and others 'became, in a sense, passive accessories to the most terrible crime in human history'.[1] In this play, *Kristallnacht* and the Holocaust more broadly symbolise the guilt of the world – not only for the Holocaust – though characters struggle to articulate precisely what they are guilty of.

As he acknowledged in writing *The Crucible*, Miller felt a deep affinity for the Puritans, and the guilt that pervades his plays has more in common with a Christian notion of original sin than with anything in the Jewish tradition. The title of his post-Holocaust play *After the Fall*, despite Miller's citing of Camus, refers to the story of a paradise lost – Adam and Eve's fall from innocence and expulsion from the Garden of Eden – and the notion that human nature is both inherently guilty and averse to taking responsibility. In this spirit, at the end of *Broken Glass*, Hyman urges Gellburg not only to forgive his wife but also 'to forgive yourself, I guess. And the Jews. And while you're at it, you can throw in the goyim.' In short, everybody is guilty and in need of forgiveness. But this universalising of guilt and the need for atonement runs counter to the Jewish tradition which insists on identifying and atoning for specific sins and on the

[1] Haskell Lookstein, *Were We Our Brothers' Keepers? The Public Response of American Jews to the Holocaust, 1938–1944* (New York: Hartmore House, 1985), 3.

obligation of those who are importuned to grant forgiveness and move on. Gellburg seems to be referring to his whole life, not a particular failing, when he finally shouts, 'God almighty, Sylvia forgive me!' And she replies, 'There's nothing to blame!' Of course, Gellburg has been to blame for compelling her to give up a job she enjoyed, for striking her on one occasion, for failing to love her as she deserved, and for other sins. In neglecting to respond substantively to his apology, she effectively dooms him. When Gellburg apologises to his boss, Stanton Case, the latter responds evasively, 'What's happening?' The inability of either Sylvia or Case to acknowledge or to forgive Gellburg when he does apologise suggests a Puritanical ethos, not a Jewish one. Both scenes end in his heart attacks, an indication, in the play's psychoanalytic vocabulary, that Gellburg is unconsciously impelled to punish his own misdeeds internally, as his conscience or super-ego inflicts him with debilitating feelings of guilt. The heart attacks symbolise this internal, self-inflicted or neurotic violence. The play posits an analogy between Gellburg's persecution of Sylvia and the Nazi persecution of the Jews, and it punishes him terribly for it.

Often Miller represents guilt as a crushing form of paralysis that must be overcome to perform moral action in the world. At the conclusion of *Incident at Vichy*, the Jewish psychiatrist Leduc tells the Austrian prince Von Berg, 'It's not your guilt I want, it's your responsibility' (289). In a 1984 interview Miller said that 'guilt is a sense of unusable responsibility; it's a responsibility that can't be expressed, that can't be utilised for one reason or another [...] it is a way of self-paralysis.'[1] Nonetheless, Miller's Holocaust plays have sometimes drawn criticism for failing to acknowledge the specificity of the crimes or to delineate responsibility. In a perceptive article, Leslie Epstein faulted *Incident at Vichy* for its abstraction of individuals.[2] He cites the German

[1] Quoted in Steven R. Centola, 'The Will to Live: An Interview with Arthur Miller' (1984), in Roudané, ed., *Conversations with Arthur Miller*, 356.
[2] Leslie Epstein, 'The Unhappiness of Arthur Miller', *Triquarterly*, Summer 1965, pp. 172–3.

philosopher Karl Jaspers's *Question of German Guilt*, which argues that to 'pronounce a group criminally, morally or metaphysically guilty is an error akin to the laziness and arrogance of average, uncritical thinking'. Leduc suggests – as Gellburg does in *Broken Glass* – that all gentiles hate the Jews. Miller has written a morality play that is perhaps more sentimental than it is pedagogical.

Miller's plays also speak to historically contingent attitudes about the role of guilt in morality. *Broken Glass* is a history play (a period piece like *The Crucible*) that enters into dialogue with a contentious debate about guilt for the Holocaust that became prevalent decades after the war. Guilt can be a productive emotion if it leads to reparation. But a pathological conscience can be tyrannical, sadistic and cruel. Sigmund Freud exercised an enormous influence on American writers of Miller's generation. He saw 'the sense of guilt as the most important problem in the development of civilization and [showed] that the price we pay for our advance in civilization is a loss of happiness through the heightening of the sense of guilt.'[1] Miller's indebtedness to Freud is particularly evident in the psychoanalytic structure of his Holocaust plays. Leduc in *Incident at Vichy*, for example, is a psychoanalyst who studied at the Psychoanalytic Institute in Vienna. In *After the Fall* the 'action takes place in the mind, thought, and memory' of the protagonist, and in *Broken Glass* the therapy is conducted by the amateur psychoanalyst, Dr Hyman. In all of these plays characters talk through memories of life-altering events and struggle with competing instincts of life and destruction, love (or sex) and death.

In *Broken Glass* Gellburg feels profoundly guilty for losing his boss a property he coveted, in spite of the fact that Gellburg did nothing wrong; on the contrary, he actively researched the site and followed a hunch conscientiously. But he made a mistake. Case's cold, unforgiving response drives the insecure Gellburg to greater and greater heights

[1] Sigmund Freud, *Civilization and Its Discontents*, trans. and ed. James Strachey (New York: W.W. Norton and Co., 1961), 97.

of guilt, and these feeling are coupled with his sense of real or imagined guilt for his wife's condition. Gellburg's insecurity, bound up with his sense of guilt, comes down to being fearful of the loss of love, whether of his wife or of his boss or, more broadly, of secular America; in short, his character manifests a Freudian model of the sense of guilt as a social anxiety. 'Say, you're not blaming this on me, are you?' Gellburg asks Hyman; to which Hyman replies, 'What's the good of blame?' – a rhetorical question, but one the play wants us to think seriously about. What *is* the good of blame? In fact, the play *does* blame Gellburg for Sylvia's plight. As Gellburg's personal and professional lives unravel simultaneously in Case's office, like Willy Loman's in *Death of a Salesman*, all he can think of is that he has been found guilty of being a Jew. 'This is not fair!' he shouts at Case and finally collapses. But Case has said nothing and appears bewildered by Gellburg's outburst. Like Willy, Phillip has internalised the authority he attributes to his boss and the aggression that he has directed towards others. He has become the victim of his own destructive impulses, his guilty conscience. In the following scene at the Gellburgs' house, Margaret says to Sylvia, 'I hope you're not blaming yourself', and her sister Harriet insists that her husband's collapse 'could happen to anybody'. Margaret then explains her philosophy of life, which is derived from working in a pediatric ward: a person's nature is set in infancy. 'So what does that mean?' Sylvia asks. It implies that no one is responsible for his or her behaviour. 'How do you live?' Margaret responds with a fatalistic ethic: 'You draw your cards face down; you turn them over and do your best with the hand you got.'

From *All My Sons* to *Broken Glass*, Miller returns continually to the crushing force of guilt and the notion that the moral responsibility of family members must expand to include all of humanity. After the surviving son in *All My Sons*, Chris Keller, returned from fighting in the Second World War, he 'felt wrong to be alive, to open a bank-book, to drive the new car', knowing that good men had gone down sacrificing themselves for each other. In the end, he tells his father, who was guilty of selling defective parts to the Air Force, 'Once and for all you can know there's a universe of people outside and you're responsible to it, and unless you know that you threw away your son because that's why he died.' This lecture on moral responsibility, however, leads Joe Keller to commit suicide, an act of self-destruction, not reparation. Many American Jews may have felt a similar form of 'survivor guilt', and Miller acknowledged that he was the lucky beneficiary of his family's emigration from Eastern Europe. On a trip to Poland Miller realised that had his grandfathers and his father not left before the turn of the century, he would not have survived to the age of thirty. In 1947–8, Miller went to Europe. In Italy he encountered Jewish refugees waiting for a ship to what was then called Palestine: 'To this day, thinking of them there on their dark porches silently scanning the sea for their ship, unwanted by any of the civilised powers, their very presence here illegal and menaced by British diplomatic intervention, I feel myself disembodied, detached, ashamed of my stupidity, my failure to recognise myself in them' (*Timebends*, 167).

For Miller guilt was a guiding emotion. In his autobiography, he even describes feeling the 'guilt of success' after his first play, *All My Sons*, was a hit. This guilt, he believed, was reinforced by his leftist egalitarian convictions, and he says that he was unable to do much about it: 'such guilt is a protective device to conceal one's happiness at surpassing others, especially those one loves, like a brother, father, or friend. It is a kind of payment to them in the form of a pseudo-remorse' (*Timebends*, 139).

Most of Miller's plays are also steeped in sexual guilt, from the past affairs of Willy Loman in *Death of a Salesman* and John Proctor in *The Crucible* to Quentin's abandonment of Maggie in *After the Fall*. One recurring motif is the figure of the neglected or damaged woman. *Broken Glass* centres on the dysfunctional sex life of the Gellburgs, which is illuminated by the unprofessional behaviour of Dr Hyman, whose vanity prompts him to treat the beautiful Sylvia. He massages and compliments her and asks her 'to imagine that we've made love' and then reacts guiltily when Gellburg says that he doesn't understand the doctor's unprofessional display. Hyman insists to his wife that '*Nothing has happened!*' Gellburg's problems at Brooklyn Trust and Guarantee are reflected in the domestic setting, where trust and love are similarly not guaranteed. Both couples in the play struggle to achieve the basis of a true marriage and to repay emotional debts. When Gellburg expresses bewilderment at Hyman's conduct, the latter 'stands there, guilty, alarmed', as his wife enters. However, although Margaret is irritated (asking 'What is it – just new ass all the time?') and Hyman insists that he hasn't been unfaithful in a decade or more, she merely concludes that he 'loves the truth' too much. It is hard not to see Margaret's absolution of Hyman as an act of wish-fulfilment.

Jewish self-hatred

The disparaging term 'self-hating Jew' refers to an anti-Semitic person who is Jewish. Its use implies that a person has betrayed his or her own identity. The founder of modern Zionism, Theodor Herzl, used the term 'anti-Semite of Jewish origin' against Jews who disagreed with Jewish aspirations for nationalism. But the term 'Jewish self-hatred' gained currency in 1930 when Theodor Lessing used it for the title of his book *Der Jüdische Selbsthass*. In the United States it was introduced as a common English term by the German-Jewish immigrant Kurt Lewin, and it came to define contentious debates about Jewish American identity in the post-war decades. The most influential academic book on the subject has been Sander Gilman's 1990 *Jewish Self-Hatred: Anti-Semitism and the Hidden Language of the Jews*.[1]

[1] Herzl used the phrase 'anti-Semite of Jewish origin' in his 1896 book *Der Judenstaat* (*The Jewish State*), which launched political Zionism. See Paul Reitter, 'Zionism and the Rhetoric of Jewish Self-Hatred', *Germanic Review*, vol. 83, no. 4, Fall 2008, pp. 343–64, and Susan A. Glenn, 'The Vogue of Jewish Self-Hatred in Post-World War II America', *Jewish Social Studies*, vol. 12, no. 3, Spring/Summer 2006, pp. 95–136.

However, Jewish 'self-hatred' is a notion that dates back to the nineteenth century when Orthodox Jews disapproved of Reform Jews, mostly in Germany, because the latter identified more with German nationalism and Protestant social norms than with what they considered to be traditional Judaism. On the other hand, the more assimilationist German Jews regarded the Eastern Europeans as 'bad' Jews, from whom they wished to distinguish themselves. Gellburg expresses the complexity of this double-edged attitude from an American perspective in *Broken Glass* when he says, 'German Jews can be pretty . . . you know . . . (*Pushes his nose with his forefinger.*) Not that they're pushy like the ones from Poland or Russia.' He has problems with both the highly assimilated Jews of German descent and the 'bad' Jew of Eastern European descent. Gellburg reflects social divisions within the Jewish community. He both loathes and identifies with the old Eastern European figure of the Jew with the sidelocks and the black hat. Gellburg's obsession with his own otherness (e.g., his 'Jewish face') draws upon negative images of the Jew in European and American culture – books, newspapers, even medical literature – that he has internalised. The language of self-hatred in the play is reflected in the motif of the mirror.

> **Hyman** All right, you want the truth? Do you? Look in the mirror sometime!
>
> **Gellburg** . . . In the mirror!
>
> **Hyman** You hate yourself, that's what's scaring her [Sylvia] to death. That's my opinion. How's it possible I don't know, but I think you helped paralyze her with this 'Jew, Jew, Jew' coming out of your mouth and the same time she reads it in the paper and it's coming out of the radio day and night? (82–3)

This revealing passage, which lays the central problem of the play (Sylvia's paralysis) at the feet of Jewish self-hatred, implies that Gellburg's problem with Jews does not come out of nowhere, or at least not only from himself; it also comes from the images and language of the media at home and abroad. Furthermore, in this dialogue between two Jewish men, it represents the tradition of the self-critical Jew and the paradoxical logic that Hyman, the one who accuses the other of being a self-hating Jew, may himself be a self-hating Jew, as Gellburg hints later when he wonders why the atheistic, horseback-riding doctor married a non-Jewish woman. As Sander Gilman writes, 'The language of the other, the mirror of the world it perceives about it, is permeated with the rhetoric of self-hatred. It takes its discourse, its mode of self-description, from the world about it, and that language is saturated with the imagined projection of the Other' (Gilman, 13). Gellburg and Sylvia discover images of themselves in the newspapers of 1938, in bearded Jews crawling the streets and being jeered at by others. It is in these images that they discover their 'Jewishness' – though they respond differently – and in the Jewish/Nazi relationship they find an ugly analogy for their own marriage.

In Gellburg's character, the play traffics in stereotypes of the feminised and sexually impotent Jewish man. In Miller's own terms of contrast, he imagined himself when a boy as 'no sallow Talmud scholar', the weak or emasculate Jew, but as one of numerous American heroes of 'athletic verve and military courage' (*Timebends*, 62). Jews were commonly depicted as bookish, urban and hysterical. In this respect, Gellburg follows the characters portrayed by Woody Allen, Saul Bellow, Phillip Roth and their precursors dating back to the early nineteenth century. But Gellburg must also be understood in relation to the stereotypical 'good Jew' of Holocaust literature, Anne Frank, the image of the Jew as 'positive' victim, the Jew who deserved to be saved because she didn't seem too 'Jewish'. Of course, Anne Frank became the good Jew by becoming first a dead Jew. *Broken Glass* deploys the polar definition of the 'self-hating' Jew – good Jew versus bad Jew – as Gellburg veers between his desire to pull a *tallis* over his head and his desire to become an assimilated American (as Anne Frank was assimilated Dutch). He internalises the charges of anti-Semitic rhetoric and projects these charges on to others labelled as Jews.

Ironically, Hyman accuses Gellburg of self-hatred for continually drawing attention to the fact that he is a Jew.

Fragmentation

The title *Broken Glass* indicates not only the historical event, *Kristallnacht*, that is central to the play, but also a broader theme of brokenness or fragmentation, starting with the Gellburgs' fragmented or broken marriage, broken trusts at work, and the fragmentation of individual lives and social structures in the historical events of the late 1930s, from the Depression to the Spanish Civil War and the breaking up of Europe in the face of Nazi aggression. The 'broken glass' of the title, suggested by the director David Thacker, also evokes an important metaphor of the Jewish mystical tradition involving the shattering of cosmic vessels and the scattering of shards of evil throughout the world. The related notion of *tikkun olam* involves the repairing of those vessels by righteous acts. It is unlikely that Miller had this specific expression in mind – he was not a practising Jew – but many Jews, who turned from their religious traditions to socialism or communism, may have redirected those traditional obligations. The phrase *tikkun olam*, which literally means to repair or perfect the world, found its way into secular forms of expression that didn't seem religious at all.

Beyond the smashing of Jewish storefronts in Hitler's Reich, the 'broken glass' of the title also refers to the breaking of the glass under the *chupah*, the wedding canopy, at the conclusion of the Jewish marriage ceremony, linking marriage, by some accounts, to the destruction of the Temple in Jerusalem. In this sense, breaking the glass identifies the married couple with the history and destiny of the Jewish people. In doing so, it relates the private, domestic covenant of marriage to a national tragedy, as Miller does in his play. Insofar as it is the groom who breaks the glass, it also suggests a moment of, perhaps, transitory or illusory male power (he gets to 'put his foot down' at least this once). Some have even linked it to the bride's loss of virginity, the breaking of the hymen. But the meaning of the ritual is disputed. Another interpretation holds that people need to remember those who are suffering in their moments of greatest joy, and this reading hints at a historical allegory especially for American Jews, wedded for the most part in peace, prosperity and security to a new homeland, not to forget their less fortunate cousins in faraway countries. Broken glass might also suggest, more simply, the wreckage following a domestic squabble. Although it is impossible to say whether Miller had any of these traditions or interpretations in mind, the evocative title of a play about a marriage suggests that the play, like the broken glass, is open to multiple interpretations.

The theme of fragmentation is also reflected in the form of the drama. Rather than unfolding like a 'well-made' play in a pattern of exposition, complication, crisis and denouement, *Broken Glass* is episodic, made up of eleven short scenes or conversations that often seem disjointed or directionless, as the speakers probe each other's hidden motivations. The conversations do not proceed in a linear or cause-and-effect pattern, and characters become confused as they trigger emotional reactions in each other by twists and turns in the dialogue. For instance, after Gellburg and the supposedly scientific Dr Hyman provoke each other, Hyman ends up complaining, 'What are you driving at, I don't understand this conversation.' The 'determined scientific idealist' finds his diagnostic powers thwarted by deep and unconscious impulses, his own included. The episodic form reflects the associative structure of memory explored by psychoanalysis, which digs into the patient's past in order to understand a present malady.

Genre

Miller's method for addressing social issues in *Broken Glass* draws on a tradition of drama that goes back to the mid-nineteenth century. At the University of Michigan he studied drama with Kenneth T. Rowe, who taught playwriting with an emphasis on form that influenced Miller's work. In his Michigan seminars and in his influential book *Write That Play!* Rowe devoted considerable attention to an analysis of Ibsen's *A Doll's House* and to Greek tragedy. During that same period Miller saw a production of *A Doll's House* on Broadway that affected him deeply, and his indebtedness to Ibsen has been widely noted. (He also wrote an adaptation of Ibsen's *An Enemy of the People*, which centres on the need for individuals to take social responsibility.) A crucial aspect of Ibsen's dramatic method that informs *Broken Glass* is the way he uses material that happened before the play began not simply to introduce a new conflict but as the play's main subject. Bringing the past to life or showing how it bears on the present is the essence of the play. This technique goes back to Sophocles' *Oedipus*, but Ibsen used it in slowly unfolding the past to tell a story about the hidden realities of everyday, middle-class life. Those realities are interpersonal.

Like *A Doll's House*, *Broken Glass* is a play about a woman trapped in an unhappy marriage, though she does not at first seem to realise that she is trapped. Both plays involve a love triangle which includes husband, wife and family doctor. Both show how people internalise the rhetoric and assumptions of their social world: what it means to be a 'good' wife and mother or husband and provider. Ibsen, too, is preoccupied with the tension between free will and determinism, the way people are shaped by a genetic inheritance or identity or whether they can assert their own selfhood in the present. In *Broken Glass*, Miller employs psychoanalysis as a way of unpacking the past in the present, but his use of the doctor as the central figure to do so is highly conventional. Furthermore, it manifests the anti-theatrical prejudice of dramatic realism: the idea that people should stop playing roles and discover the truth about themselves. Sylvia literally embodies this anti-theatrical logic in her refusal or inability to act as her husband or doctor desire, and the play punishes Gellburg's theatrical conceptions of identity – whether it means acting the Jew or the Republican or anything that seems false to the 'human'.

The thesis play developed in the nineteenth century to deal with controversial social concerns in a realistic manner. Thesis plays commonly required a character to serve as presenter and preacher and to function as the author's mouthpiece. Known in French as the *raisonneur*, many modern plays have given this role to a doctor, who generally brings a scientific approach to problems yet also has a personal involvement with the characters which suggests the limits of rationality. While in some ways doctors such as those in Ibsen's *A Doll's House* and Chekhov's *Ivanov* serve as precursors for Dr Hyman in *Broken Glass*, Miller's play differs in its treatment. Instead of being a marginal character, Dr Hyman is central to the play's action and is its key moraliser, and though Hyman's wife Margaret seems occasionally bemused, the play does not deflate or question his self-importance and 'scientific idealism'.

Characters

Phillip Gellburg

A 'self-hating Jew' in his late forties, Phillip Gellburg is head of the Mortgage Department at the Brooklyn Guarantee and Trust Company and answerable only to the WASP (White Anglo-Saxon Protestant) owner. He is the only Jew ever to have been hired by the company and proud of it. Gellburg evaluates properties and establishes the terms of mortgages. The ideas of 'guarantee' and 'trust' resonate at a deeper level, as Gellburg loses the trust of his boss and, he fears, the guarantee of his status in America. He has internalised the mirage of the 'typical Jew' as a reality. His anxieties are self-fulfilling and represent a double-bind: he makes a mistake at work by trying to be too clever. He overreacts to slights and anticipates prejudice, which only antagonises his prejudiced boss and alienates his wife. He wants to erase his origins but succeeds only in drawing attention to them. He is a Republican (most Jews were and are Democrats) and prejudiced against immigrants, but his politics draw attention to his difference. Gellburg's inability to 'be a man' in the bedroom reinforces the stereotype of Jews as physically weak and, given the practice of circumcision, not quite 'whole' men. As the theatre critic Vincent Canby writes, Gellburg 'is a small man but he's a gigantic mess. Half of him is as anti-Semitic as [his boss] Stanton Case . . . The other, only vaguely recognised half is the bewildered son of immigrants, a first-generation Jewish American trying to assimilate' (*New York Times*, 1 May 1994).

Sylvia Gellburg

The wife of Phillip, Sylvia Gellburg, is a beautiful and talented woman, paralysed from the waist down. Intellectually curious but with little formal education, she is a constant reader of books and newspapers, and 'remarkably well informed'. Before her marriage, she was head bookkeeper for a company in Long Island City. She loved work and having people depend on her. Her husband says that if she were a man she could have run the Federal Reserve and that he can talk to her as to a man. These comments reinforce a sense of gender confusion and sexual dysfunction in the Gellburg home; Sylvia's temporary inability to use her legs is parallel to Phillip's inability to use his penis. Both suggest castration anxieties. Her husband compelled her to give up her job, and Sylvia represents the frustrations of a generation of women who came of age between first- and second-wave feminism. She is both a comfortable American housewife and a victim of domestic abuse. She was paralysed and confined, figuratively, long before her legs gave out. Her predicament resembles that of many frustrated women. Miller claimed that he knew an actual woman who suffered 'hysterical paralysis' and whose husband dressed in black (like Gellburg), but Sylvia is an emblematic figure, less realistic than allegorical.

Through her the play brings together public and private concerns. Her paralysis also suggests the failures of American Jews in the face of the European Holocaust, Western appeasement and American neutrality, as German forces penetrated Europe in the late thirties. Although her condition represents American inaction, she is also a figure for the victims of an oppressive anti-Semitic regime (in her case represented by her husband). In Sylvia, we see how an inner life reflects larger social and historical events. The married couple is a microcosm that channels larger social pathologies.

Dr Harry Hyman

Hyman is a 'determined scientific idealist', implying a capacity to regard his existence from two standpoints and, thus, to perfect the baser material reality by reference to the higher, idealistic one. Hyman's name (pronounced high-man) indicates that he is the opposite of Miller's best-known character, Willy Loman; this sense of opposition is enhanced by the fact that Gellburg – Hyman's opposite in the play – resembles Willy Loman. A successful physician and Casanova, Hyman's high opinion of himself is shared by most of the other characters in the play, though he lacks the ambition that his wife Margaret believes would land him a practice on Park Avenue. But Hyman is a socialist, and he explains at one point that he likes to think carefully before he speaks, comparing himself to the literary doctors Somerset Maugham and Anton Chekhov.

In Greek mythology, Hymen was a god of marriage and attended every wedding (Shakespeare employs the figure in *As You Like It*). If the god Hymen wasn't present, legend had it, the marriage would prove disastrous. (Hyman's references to the Ancient Greek god of medicine and to the Greek etymology of 'hysteria' invite the reader to make similar inferences about his name.) The hymen is also the mucous membrane on a woman's vagina, which has a long history in medicine and the popular imagination, including the myth that examining the hymen could prove a woman's virginity or that damage to it could cause 'hysteria' (Dr Hyman claims that Sylvia suffers a 'hysterical paralysis'). The name also has a Jewish provenance. Miller's uncle was named Hymie, a name that remains a classic anti-Semitic epithet. In short, Hyman's overdetermined masculinity in the play is balanced by a name that was not only common among Jews but that also evokes mythic aspects of female anatomy, suggesting the complex interplay between the masculine/feminine terms in the play. There is a long tradition of depicting Jewish men as impaired, limping and feminised, not completely male. Yet all of the women in the play, from Sylvia and her sister Harriet to Hyman's wife Margaret, refer to his sexual potency, and he gives evidence of seductive power on stage with both Margaret and Sylvia. Hyman's assertion of both his masculinity and his secular humanism are related to what he is asserting it against: a figure embodied by Gellburg but also latent in himself.

Margaret Hyman

Margaret is the 'shiksa' or non-Jewish wife and medical assistant of Dr Hyman. A vivacious Midwesterner who came east, she met Hyman when he was an intern at Mount Sinai Hospital. Margaret is a limited character, but she offers a complicated, even contradictory, comment on the sources of identity. On the one hand, in her marriage she represents the idea that identity can be freely chosen, a matter of consent rather than descent. Intermarriage between Jews and gentiles was frowned upon (and rare) in the 1930s, as Miller has noted regarding his own first marriage to non-Jewish Mary Grace Slattery. In choosing Hyman, Margaret indicates that identity is not fixed. When Gellburg pretentiously and improbably claims that his family was 'originally' from Finland, where few Jews ever lived, Margaret casually answers that hers, equally improbably, came from Lithuania; it is a way of bursting Gellburg's bubble and of hinting that it doesn't matter where one's family came from. On the other hand, in the penultimate scene of the play, attempting to absolve Sylvia's feelings of guilt, Margaret says that people's characters are determined before birth: 'each one has twenty thousand years of the human race backed up behind him . . . and you expect to change him?' This remark, suggesting that character is formed totally by descent rather than consent, baffles Sylvia.

Harriet
Sylvia's sister Harriet is younger by a couple of years. She helps to look after Sylvia, taking care of her housework and shopping. Much less intense and thoughtful than her sister, she is a conventional housewife. Another limited character, her main function is to set off Sylvia's qualities of intellectual curiosity, frustration with her lot, political engagement and empathy for strangers. She provides additional evidence that women in general are attracted to Hyman.

Stanton Wylie Case
Mr Case is Gellburg's boss and the President of Brooklyn Guarantee. Case represents the American WASP establishment. His yacht won the America's Cup. He wants to purchase an annexe for the Harvard Club, implying that as a member of the Northeastern elite he went to Harvard, which restricted the number of Jewish students admitted to the university from the 1920s to the late 1930s. Case's fifty-year-old company, however, depends on its key Jewish employee, Gellburg. He is a two-dimensional character without psychological depth. He comes close to being a standard capitalist villain. His main purpose in the play is to serve as an occasion for Gellburg's Jewish self-hatred. He appears oblivious to his own prejudices when Gellburg finally becomes exercised at his unconscious but deep-seeded bigotry.

Key productions

Broken Glass premiered at the Long Wharf Theatre in New Haven, Connecticut, on 1 March 1994, with Amy Irving as Sylvia, Ron Rifkin as Gellburg and Ron Silver as Hyman, before moving to Broadway, where Silver was replaced by

David Dukes. Miller's producer Robert Whitehead insisted on doing the play in New York rather than London because he was concerned that if the production turned out badly or was poorly reviewed in Britain, he would have difficulty raising money to do it in New York. The opening on 24 April 1994 at the Booth Theatre marked Miller's return to Broadway after an absence of fourteen years, but the play ran only two months and opened to mixed reviews. Although Amy Irving was acclaimed for her performance as Sylvia, the critic David Richards complained in the *New York Times* that the play was predictable, 'all talk and fumbling confession'. The set was designed by Santo Loquasto on a sleek turntable (doctor's office, bedroom, board room), with a shared visual motif of white tiles. Original cello music was composed for the production by William Bolcom.

The Royal National Theatre in London scheduled *Broken Glass* for its Lyttleton Theatre under the precise direction of David Thacker, who enhanced the drama's general atmosphere of foreboding. Miller revised the play immediately after it closed in New York; so the text of the final script was very different from the one used in the American production. Considerably strengthened, the play won the Olivier Award as the Best New Play of the year for the 1994–5 London season. British theatre critics argued that the New York failure had been that of American audiences rather than of Miller's play. The Royal National Theatre production featured Margot Leicester as limpid-eyed Sylvia, Henry Goodman as a prickly, impatient Phillip and Ken Stott as a rumpled, chain-smoking Hyman. The play was staged in a dreamlike set designed by Shelagh Keegan that suggested the fragility of the characters' safety in New York. The triangular stage tapered sharply towards the back, where the cellist played mournfully between scenes, and the walls were sheets of glass. After its sell-out run at the Royal National Theatre, *Broken Glass* transferred to the West End for a ten-week season. Thacker also went on to direct a film version in 1996, which was produced by the BBC and aired in America on 'Masterpiece Theatre'. The film employed a strong cast, with Leicester and Goodman again as the struggling Gellburgs, and Mandy

Patinkin as a burly Hyman, and it 'opened out' the action by showing events which are only reported in the original dialogue, such as Hyman riding on horseback on the beach, Gellburg foreclosing an apartment and dark, haunting images of Nazi violence blended with Sylvia's dreams. It also introduced new minor characters, such as the Gellburgs' nephew David.

Shortly after the London triumph, the play returned to the United States, where it was produced outside Washington, DC, at the Olney Theatre Center, in a co-production with the Rep Stage Company. In this production James Kronzer's revolving set, lit in evocative shadows, was composed of dark wood and panes of broken glass. The co-directors Jim Petosa and Halo Wines created an intensely acted show with Ed Gero playing Phillip as 'a black hole of angst', in the words of the *Washington Times*. Subsequently, the play has had a long and varied production history, from a 1998 production in Australia, to Joseph Chaikin's elegantly directed production in Atlanta, Georgia, to productions at Burbank's Victory Theatre in Los Angeles and the Winnipeg Jewish Theatre in Canada in 2006. In 2009 a spare production was put on at the Blackwood Little Theatre in South Wales, and it was staged several times in 2010, including one version at the Walnut Street Theatre in Philadelphia, and another in London at the Tricycle Theatre, starring Antony Sher. In October 2010, the *New York Times* described the Tricycle Theatre production, directed by Iqbal Khan and intended for a commercial transfer to the West End, as the 'best yet'. With a super essemble around Sher and a mood-setting onstage cellist, this staging sharpened the drama's focus and did 'nothing less than put the Jewish psyche on trial'. Though critics have sometimes found the symbolism heavy-handed and the tone moralistic, most have generally agreed that in performance it conveys impressive moral power.

Further Reading

Works by Arthur Miller

Arthur Miller Plays, 6 vols (vol. 1: *All My Sons*, *Death of a Salesman*, *The Crucible*, *A Memory of Two Mondays*, *A View from the Bridge*; vol. 2: *The Misfits*, *After the Fall*, *Incident at Vichy*, *The Price*, *Creation of the World*, *Playing for Time*; vol. 3: *The American Clock*, *The Archbishop's Ceiling*, *Two-Way Mirror*; vol. 4: *The Golden Years*, *The Man Who Had All the Luck*, *I Can't Remember Anything*, *Clara*; vol. 5: *The Last Yankee*, *The Ride Down Mount Morgan*, *Almost Everybody Wins*; vol. 6: *Broken Glass*, *Mr Peters' Connections*, *Resurrection Blues*, *Finishing the Picture*), London: Methuen Drama, 1988–2009

After the Fall, with commentary and notes by Brenda Murphy. London: Methuen Drama, 2011

All My Sons, with commentary and notes by Toby Zinman. London: Methuen Drama, 2010

The Crucible, with commentary and notes by Susan Abbotson. London: Methuen Drama, 2010

Death of a Salesman, with commentary and notes by Enoch Brater. London: Methuen Drama, 2010

The Last Yankee, with commentary and notes by Katherine Egerton. London: Methuen Drama, 2011

A Memory of Two Mondays, with commentary and notes by Joshua Polster. London: Methuen Drama, 2011

The Price, with commentary and notes by Jane K. Dominik. London. Methuen Drama, 2011

A View From the Bridge, with commentary and notes by Steve Marino. London: Methuen Drama, 2010

Echoes Down the Corridor: Collected Essays 1944–2000, ed. Steven R. Centola. London: Methuen, 2000

The Theatre Essays of Arthur Miller, ed. Robert A. Martin. London: Methuen, 1994

Timebends: A Life. London: Methuen, 1987

Books on Arthur Miller

Bigsby, Christopher. *Arthur Miller: A Critical Study*. Cambridge: Cambridge University Press 2005

Bigsby, Christopher. *Arthur Miller: The Definitive Biography*. London: Weidenfeld and Nicolson, 2008

Bigsby, Christopher, ed. *Arthur Miller and Company: Arthur Miller Talks About His Work in the Company of Actors, Designers, Directors, Reviewers and Writers*. London: Methuen Drama and the Arthur Miller Centre for American Studies, 1990

Bigsby, Christopher, ed. *Remembering Arthur Miller*. London: Methuen in association with the Arthur Miller Centre for American Studies, 2005

Brater, Enoch. *Arthur Miller: A Playwright's Life and Works*. London: Thames and Hudson, 2005

Brater, Enoch, ed. *Arthur Miller's America: Theater and Culture in a Time of Change*. Ann Arbor: University of Michigan Press, 2005

Brater, Enoch, ed. *Arthur Miller's Global Theater*. Ann Arbor: University of Michigan Press, 2007

Centola, Steve. *Arthur Miller in Conversation*. Dallas: Northouse and Northouse, 1993

Centola, Steven R. and Michelle Cirulli, eds. *The Critical Response to Arthur Miller*. Westport, CT: Praeger, 2006

Goldstein, Lawrence, ed. 'A Special Issue: Arthur Miller', *Michigan Quarterly Review*. Ann Arbor: University of Michigan, 1998

Gottfried, Martin. *Arthur Miller: His Life and Work*. New York: Da Capo Press, 2003

Langteau, Paula. *Miller and Middle America: Essays on Arthur Miller and the American Experience*. Lanham, MD: University Press of America, 2007

Roudané, Matthew, ed. *Conversations with Arthur Miller*. Jackson, MI and London: University of Mississippi Press, 1987

Welland, Dennis. *Miller: The Playwright*. London: Methuen, 1985

Background

Bigsby, Christopher. *Remembering and Imagining the Holocaust: The Chain of Memory*. Cambridge: Cambridge University Press, 2006

Diner, Hasia R. *The Jews of the United States, 1654–2000.* Berkeley: University of California Press, 2004

Finlay, W. M. L. 'Pathologizing Dissent: Identity Politics, Zionism and the "Self-Hating Jew" '. *British Journal of Social Psychology*, vol. 44, no. 2, pp. 201–22, June 2005

Gilman, Sander L. *Jewish Self-Hatred: Anti-Semitism and the Hidden Language of the Jews*. Baltimore, MD: Johns Hopkins University Press, 1990

Lerman, Antony. 'Jewish Self-Hatred: Myth or Reality?' *Jewish Quarterly*, Summer 2008

Lewin, Kurt. 'Self-Hatred Among Jews'. *Contemporary Jewish Record*, June 1941. Reprinted in Kurt Lewin, *Resolving Social Conflicts: Selected Papers on Group Dynamics*. New York: Harper & Row, 1948

Mamet, David. *The Wicked Son: Anti-Semitism, Self-Hatred, and the Jews*. New York: Schocken Books, 2006

Novick, Peter. *The Holocaust in American Life*. New York: Mariner Books, 2000

Plunka, Gene A. *Holocaust Drama: The Theater of Atrocity*. Cambridge: Cambridge University Press, 2009

Sarna, Jonathan D. *American Judaism: A History*. New Haven, CN: Yale University Press, 2004

Schumacker, Claude. *Staging the Holocaust: The Shoah in Drama and Performance*. Cambridge: Cambridge University Press, 1998

Broken Glass

Broken Glass received its British premiere at the Royal National Theatre on 4 August 1994, with the following cast:

Phillip Gellburg	Henry Goodman
Sylvia Gellburg	Margot Leicester
Dr Harry Hyman	Ken Stott
Margaret Hyman	Sally Edwards
Harriet	Julia Swift
Stanton Case	Ed Bishop

Directed by David Thacker
Designed by Shelagh Keegan
Lighting by Alan Burrett
Music by Gary Yershon and Andrea Hess
Cellist Andrea Hess

Characters

Phillip Gellburg
Sylvia Gellburg
Dr Harry Hyman
Margaret Hyman
Harriet
Stanton Case

The play takes place in Brooklyn in the last days of November, 1938.

A lone cellist is discovered, playing a simple tune. The tune finishes. Light goes out on the cellist and rises on . . .

Scene One

Office of **Dr Harry Hyman** *in his home. Alone on stage* **Phillip Gellburg**, *a slender, intense man in his late forties, waits in perfect stillness, legs crossed. He is in a black suit, black tie and shoes and white shirt.* **Margaret Hyman**, *the doctor's wife, enters. She is fair, lusty, energetic, carries pruning shears.*

Margaret He'll be right with you, he's just changing. Can I get you something? Tea?

Gellburg (*faint reprimand*) He said five o'clock sharp.

Margaret He was held up in the hospital, that new union's pulled a strike,* imagine? A strike in a hospital? It's incredible. And his horse went lame.

Gellburg His horse?

Margaret He rides on Ocean Parkway* every afternoon.

Gellburg (*attempting easy familiarity*) Oh yes, I heard about that . . . it's very nice. You're Mrs Hyman?

Margaret I've nodded to you on the street for years now, but you're too preoccupied to notice.

Gellburg (*a barely hidden boast*) Lot on my mind, usually. (*A certain amused loftiness.*) – So you're his nurse, too.

Margaret We met in Mount Sinai* when he was interning. He's lived to regret it. (*She laughs in a burst.*)

Gellburg That's some laugh you've got there. I sometimes hear you all the way down the block to my house.

Margaret Can't help it, my whole family does it. I'm originally from Minnesota.* It's nice to meet you finally, Mr Goldberg.

Gellburg It's Gellburg, not Goldberg.

Margaret Oh, I'm sorry.

Gellburg G-e-l-l-b-u-r-g. It's the only one in the phone book.

Margaret It does sound like Goldberg.

Gellburg But it's not, it's Gellberg. (*A distinction.*) We're from Finland originally.

Margaret Oh! We came from Lithuania . . . Kazauskis?*

Gellburg (*put down momentarily*) Don't say.

Margaret (*trying to charm him to his ease*) Ever been to Minnesota?

Gellburg New York State's the size of France, what would I go to Minnesota for?

Margaret Nothing. Just there's a lot of Finns there.

Gellburg Well, there's Finns all over.

Margaret (*defeated, shows the clipper*) . . . I'll get back to my roses. Whatever it is I hope you'll be feeling better.

Gellburg It's not me.

Margaret Oh. 'Cause you seem a little pale.

Gellburg Me? – I'm always this color. It's my wife.

Margaret I'm sorry to hear that, she's a lovely woman. It's nothing serious, is it?

Gellburg He's just had a specialist put her through some tests, I'm waiting to hear. I think it's got him mystified.

Margaret Well, I mustn't butt in. (*Makes to leave but can't resist.*) Can you say what it is?

Gellburg She can't walk.

Margaret What do you mean?

Gellburg (*an overtone of protest of some personal victimization*) Can't stand up. No feeling in her legs. – I'm sure it'll pass, but it's terrible.

Margaret But I only saw her in the grocery . . . can't be more than ten days ago . . .

Gellburg It's nine days today.

Margaret But she's such a wonderful-looking woman. Does she have fever?

Gellburg No.

Margaret Thank God, then it's not polio.*

Gellburg No, she's in perfect health otherwise.

Margaret Well Harry'll get to the bottom of it if anybody can. They call him from everywhere for opinions, you know . . . Boston, Chicago . . . By rights he ought to be on Park Avenue if he only he had the ambition, but he always wanted a neighborhood practice. Why, I don't know – we never invite anybody, we never go out, all our friends are in Manhattan. But it's his nature, you can't fight a person's nature. Like me for instance, I like to talk and I like to laugh. You're not much of a talker are you.

Gellburg (*purse-mouthed smile*) When I can get a word in edgewise.

Margaret (*burst of laughter*) Ha! – So you've got a sense of humor after all. Well, give my best to Mrs Goldberg.

Gellburg Gellbu –

Margaret (*hits her own head*) Gellburg, excuse me! – It practically sounds like Goldberg.

Gellburg No-no, look in the phonebook, it's the only one, G-e-l-l . . .

Enter **Dr Hyman**.

Margaret (*with a little wave to* **Gellberg**) Be seeing you!

Gellburg Be in good health.

Margaret *exits.*

Hymen (*in his early fifties, a determined scientific idealist. Settling behind his desk, chuckling*) She chew your ear off?!

Gellburg (*his worldly mode*) Not too bad, I've had worse.

Hyman Well, there's no way around it, women are talkers. (*Grinning familiarly.*) But try living without them, right?

Gellburg Without women?

Hymen (*he sees* **Gellberg** *has flushed; there is a short hiatus, then . . .*) Well, never mind. – I'm glad you could make it tonight, I wanted to talk to you before I see your wife again tomorrow. Smoke?

Gellburg No thanks, never have. Isn't it bad for you?

Hyman Certainly is. (*Lights a cigar.*) But more people die of rat bite, you know.

Gellburg Rat bite!

Hyman Oh yes, but they're mostly the poor, so it's not an interesting statistic. Have you seen her tonight, or did you come here from the office?

Gellburg I thought I'd see you before I went home. But I phoned her this afternoon – same thing, no change.

Hyman How's she doing with the wheelchair?

Gellburg Better, she can get herself in and out of the bed now.

Hyman Good. And she manages the bathroom?

Gellburg Oh yes. I got the maid to come in the mornings to help her take a bath, clean up . . .

Hyman Good. Your wife has a lot of courage, I admire that kind of woman. My wife is similar; I like the type.

Gellburg What type you mean?

Hyman You know – vigorous. I mean mentally and . . . you know, just generally. Moxie.*

Gellburg Oh.

Hyman Forget it, it was only a remark.

Gellburg No, you're right, I never thought of it, but she is unusually that way.

Hymen (*pause. Some prickliness here which he can't understand*) Dr Sherman's report.

Gellburg What's he say?

Hyman I'm getting to it.

Gellburg Oh. Beg your pardon.

Hyman You'll have to bear with me . . . may I call you Phillip?

Gellburg Certainly.

Hyman I don't express my thoughts very quickly, Phillip.

Gellburg Likewise. Go ahead, take your time.

Hyman People tend to overestimate the wisdom of physicians so I try to think things through before I speak to a patient.

Gellburg I'm glad to hear that.

Hyman Aesculapius stuttered, you know – ancient Greek god of medicine. But probably based on a real physician who hesitated about giving advice. Somerset Maugham stammered, studied medicine. Anton Chekhov,* great writer, also a doctor, had tuberculosis. Doctors are very often physically defective in some way, that's why they're interested in healing.

Gellburg (*impressed*) I see.

Hymen (*pause. Thinks*) I find this Adolph Hitler very disturbing. You been following him in the papers?

Gellburg Well yes, but not much. My average day in the office is ten, eleven hours.

Hyman They've been smashing the Jewish stores in Berlin all week,* you know.

Gellburg Oh yes, I saw that again yesterday.

Hyman Very disturbing. Forcing old men to scrub the sidewalks with toothbrushes. On the Kurfürstendamm,* that's equivalent to Fifth Avenue. Nothing but hoodlums in uniform.

Gellburg My wife is very upset about that.

Hyman I know, that's why I mention it. (*Hesitates.*) And how about you?

Gellburg Of course. It's a terrible thing. Why do you ask?

Hymen (*a smile*) – I don't know, I got the feeling she may be afraid she's annoying you when she talks about such things.

Gellburg Why? I don't mind. – She said she's annoying me?

Hyman Not in so many words, but . . .

Gellburg I can't believe she'd say a thing like . . .

Hyman Wait a minute, I didn't say she said it . . .

Gellburg She doesn't annoy me but what can be done about such things? The thing is, she doesn't like to hear about the other side of it.

Hyman What other side?

Gellburg It's no excuse for what's happening over there but German Jews can be pretty . . . you know . . . (*Pushes up his nose with his forefinger.*) Not that they're pushy like the ones from Poland or Russia but friend of mine's in the garment industry; these German Jews won't take an ordinary good job, you know; it's got to be pretty high up in the firm or they're insulted. And they can't even speak English.

Hyman Well I guess a lot of them were pretty important over there.

Gellburg I know, but they're supposed to be *refugees*,* aren't they? With all our unemployment you'd think they'd appreciate a little more. Latest official figure is twelve million unemployed you know, and it's probably bigger but Roosevelt* can't admit it, after the fortune he's pouring into WPA and the rest of that welfare *mishugas*.* – But she's not *annoying* me, for God's sake.

Hyman . . . I just thought I'd mention it; but it was only a feeling I had.

Gellburg I'll tell you right now, I don't run with the crowd, I see with these eyes, nobody else's.

Hyman I see that. – You're very unusual. (*Grinning.*) You almost sound like a Republican.*

Gellburg Why? – The Torah* says a Jew has to be a Democrat? I didn't get where I am by agreeing with everybody.

Hyman Well that's a good thing; you're independent. (*Nods, puffs.*) You know, what mystifies me is that the Germans I knew in Heidelberg* . . . I took my MD there . . .

Gellburg You got along with them.

Hyman Some of the finest people I ever met.

Gellburg Well, there you go.

Hyman We had a marvelous student choral group, fantastic voices; Saturday nights, we'd have a few beers and go singing through the streets . . . People'd applaud from the windows.

Gellburg Don't say . . .

Hyman I simply can't imagine those people marching into Austria, and now they say Czechoslovakia's next, and Poland . . .* But fanatics have taken Germany, I guess, and they can be brutal, you know . . .

Gellburg Listen, I sympathize with these refugees, but . . .

Hymen (*cutting him off*) I had quite a long talk with Sylvia yesterday, I suppose she told you?

Gellburg (*a tensing*) Well . . . no, she didn't mention. What about?

Hymen (*surprised by* **Sylvia***'s omission*) . . . Well, about her condition, and . . . just in passing . . . your relationship.

Gellburg (*flushing*) *My* relationship?

Hyman . . . It was just in passing.

Gellburg Why, what'd she say?

Hyman Well, that you . . . get along very well.

Gellburg Oh.

Hymen (*encouragingly, as he sees* **Gellberg***'s small tension*) I found her a remarkably well-informed woman. Especially for this neighborhood.*

Gellburg (*a pridefully approving nod; relieved that he can speak of her positively*) That's practically why we got together in the first place. I don't exaggerate, if Sylvia was a man she could have run the Federal Reserve.* You could talk to Sylvia like you talk to a man.

Hyman I'll bet.

Gellburg (*his purse-mouthed grin*) . . . Not that talking was all we did – but you turn your back on Sylvia and she's got her nose in a book or a magazine. I mean there's not one woman in ten around here could even tell you who their Congressman* is. And you can throw in the men, too. (*Pause.*) So where are we?

Hyman Dr Sherman confirms my diagnosis. I ask you to listen carefully, will you?

Gellburg (*brought up*) Of course, that's why I came.

Hyman We can find no physical reason for her inability to walk.

Gellburg No physical reason.

Hyman We are almost certain that this is a psychological condition.

Gellburg But she's numb, she has no feeling in her legs.

Hyman Yes. This is what we call an hysterical paralysis.* Hysterical doesn't mean she screams and yells . . .

Gellburg Oh, I know. It means like . . . ah . . . (*Bumbles off.*)

Hymen (*a flash of umbrage, dislike*) Let me explain what it means, okay? – Hysteria comes from the Greek word for the womb because it was thought to be a symptom of female anxiety. Of course it isn't, but that's where it comes from. People who are anxious enough or really frightened can imagine they've gone blind or deaf, for instance . . . and they really can't see or hear. It was sometimes called shell-shock during the War.*

Gellburg You mean . . . you don't mean she's . . . crazy.

Hyman We'll have to talk turkey, Phillip. If I'm going to do you any good. I'm going to have to ask you some personal questions. Some of them may sound raw, but I've only been superficially acquainted with Sylvia's family and I need to know more . . .

Gellburg She says you treated her father . . .

Hyman Briefly; a few visits shortly before he passed away. They're fine people. I hate like hell to see this happen to her, you see what I mean?

Gellburg You can tell it to me; is she crazy?

Hyman Phillip, are you? Am I? In one way or another who isn't crazy? The main difference is that our kind of crazy still allows us to walk around and tend to our business. But who knows? – People like us may be the craziest of all.

Gellburg (*scoffing grin*) Why!

Hyman Because we don't know we're nuts and the other kind does.

Gellburg I don't know about that . . .

Hyman Well, it's neither here nor there.

Gellburg I certainly don't think *I'm* nuts.

Hyman I wasn't saying that . . .

Gellburg What do you mean, then?

Hymen (*grinning*) You're not an easy man to talk to, are you.

Gellburg Why? If I don't understand I have to ask, don't I?

Hyman Yes, you're right.

Gellburg That's the way I am – they don't pay me for being easy to talk to.

Hyman You're in . . . real estate?

Gellburg I'm head of the Mortgage Department of Brooklyn Guarantee and Trust.*

Hyman Oh, that's right, she told me.

Gellburg We are the largest lender east of the Mississippi.

Hyman Really. (*Fighting deflation.*) Well, let me tell you my approach; if possible I'd like to keep her out of that whole psychiatry rigmarole. Not that I'm against it, but I think you get further faster, sometimes, with a little common sense and some plain human sympathy. Can we talk turkey? *Tuchas offen tisch,** you know any Yiddish?

Gellburg Yes, it means get your ass on the table.

Hyman Correct. So let's forget crazy and try to face the facts. We have a strong, healthy woman who has no physical ailment, and suddenly can't stand on her legs. Why?

He goes silent. **Gellberg** *shifts uneasily.*

Hyman I don't mean to embarrass you . . .

Gellburg (*an angry smile*) You're not embarrassing me. – What do you want to know?

Hymen (*sets himself then launches*) In these cases there is often a sexual element. You have relations, I imagine?

Gellburg Relations? Yes, we have relations.

Hymen (*a softening smile*) Often?

Gellburg What's that got to do with it?

Hyman Sex could be connected. You don't have to answer.

Gellburg No-no it's all right . . . I would say it depends – maybe twice, three times a week.

Hymen (*seems surprised*) Well that's good. She seems satisfied?

Gellburg (*shrugs; hostilely*) I guess she is, sure.

Hyman That was a foolish question, forget it.

Gellburg (*flushed*) Why, did she mention something about this?

Hyman Oh no, it's just something I thought of later.

Gellburg Well, I'm no Rudolph Valentino,* but I . . .

Hyman Rudolph Valentino probably wasn't either. – What about before she collapsed – was that completely out of the blue or . . . ?

Gellburg (*relieved to be off the other subject*) I tell you, looking back I wonder if something happened when they started putting all the pictures in the paper. About these Nazi carryings-on. I noticed she started . . . staring at them . . . in a very peculiar way. And . . . I don't know. It made her angry or something.

Hyman At you.

Gellburg Well . . . (*Nods, agreeing.*) in general. – Personally I don't think they should be publishing those kind of pictures.

Hyman Why not?

Gellburg She scares herself to death with them – three thousand miles away, and what does it accomplish! Except maybe put some fancy new ideas into these anti-Semites* walking around New York here . . .

Slight pause.

Hyman Tell me how she collapsed. You were going to the movies . . . ?

Gellburg (*breathing more deeply*) Yes. We were just starting down the porch steps and all of a sudden her . . . (*Difficulty; he breaks off.*)

Hyman I'm sorry but I . . .

Gellburg . . . Her legs turned to butter. I couldn't stand her up. Kept falling around like a rag doll. I had to carry her into the house. And she kept apologizing . . . ! (*He weeps; recovers.*) I can't talk about it.

Hyman It's all right.

Gellburg She's always been such a level-headed woman. (*Weeping threatens again.*) I don't know what to do. She's my life.

Hyman I'll do my best for her, Phillip, she's a wonderful woman. – Let's talk about something else. What do you do exactly?

Gellburg I mainly evaluate properties.

Hyman Whether to grant a mortgage . . .

Gellburg And how big a one and the terms.

Hyman How's the Depression* hit you?

Gellburg Well, it's no comparison with '32 to '36, let's say – we were foreclosing* left and right in those days. But we're on our feet and running.

Hyman And you head the department . . .

Gellburg Above me is only Mr Case. Stanton Wylie Case; he's chairman and president. You're not interested in boat racing?

Hyman Why?

Gellburg His yacht won the America's Cup two years ago. For the second time. The *Aurora*?

Hyman Oh yes! I think I read about . . .

Gellburg He's had me aboard twice.

Hyman Really.

Gellburg (*the grin*) The only Jew* ever set foot on that deck.

Hyman Don't say.

Gellburg In fact, I'm the only Jew ever worked for Brooklyn Guarantee in their whole history.

Hyman That so.

Gellburg Oh yes. And they go back to the 1890s. Started right out of accountancy school and moved straight up. They've been wonderful to me; it's a great firm.

A long moment as **Hyman** *stares at* **Gellberg**, *who is proudly positioned now, absorbing his poise from the evoked memories of his success. Gradually* **Gellberg** *turns to* **Hyman**.

Gellburg How could this be a mental condition?

Hyman It's unconscious; like . . . well, take yourself: I notice you're all in black. Can I ask you why?

Gellburg I've worn black since high school.

Hyman No particular reason.

Gellburg (*shrugs*) Always liked it, that's all.

Hyman Well, it's a similar thing with her; she doesn't know why she's doing this, but some very deep, hidden part of her mind is directing her to do it. You don't agree.

Gellburg I don't know.

Hyman You think she knows what she's doing?

Gellburg Well, I always liked black for business reasons.

Hyman It gives you authority?

Gellburg Not exactly authority, but I wanted to look a little older. See, I graduated high school at fifteen and I was only twenty-two when I entered the firm. But I knew what I was doing.

Hyman Then you think she's doing this on purpose?

Gellburg – Except she's numb; nobody can purposely do that, can they?

Hyman I don't think so. – I tell you, Phillip, not really knowing your wife, if you have any idea why she could be doing this to herself . . .

Gellburg I told you, I don't know.

Hyman Nothing occurs to you.

Gellburg (*an edge of irritation*) I can't think of anything.

Hyman I'll tell you a funny thing, talking to her she doesn't seem all that unhappy.

Gellburg Say! – Yes, that's what I mean. That's exactly what I mean. It's like she's almost . . . I don't know . . . enjoying herself. I mean in a way.

Hyman How could that be possible?

Gellburg Of course she apologizes for it, and for making it hard for me – you know, like I have to do a lot of the cooking now, and tending to my laundry and so on . . . I even shop for groceries and the butcher . . . and change the sheets.

He breaks off with some realization. **Hyman** *doesn't speak. A long pause.*

Gellburg You mean . . . she's doing it against me?

Hyman I don't know, what do you think?

Gellburg (*stares for a long moment, then makes to rise, obviously deeply disturbed*) I'd better be getting home. (*Lost in his own thought.*) I don't know whether to ask you this or not.

Hyman What's to lose, go ahead.

Gellburg My parents were from the old country, you know – I don't know if it was in Poland someplace or Russia* – but there was this woman who they say was . . . you know . . . gotten into by a . . . like the ghost of a dead person.

Hyman A dybbuk.*

Gellburg That's it. And it made her lose her mind and so forth. – You believe in that? They had to get a Rabbi* to pray it out of her body. But you think that's possible?

Hyman Do I think so? No. Do you?

Gellburg Oh no. It just crossed my mind.

Hyman Well I wouldn't know how to pray it out of her, so . . .

Gellburg Be straight with me – is she going to come out of this?

Hyman Well, let's talk again after I see her tomorrow. Maybe I should tell you . . . I have this unconventional approach to illness, Phillip. Especially where the mental element is involved. I believe we get sick in twos and threes, not alone as individuals. You follow me? I want you to do me a favor, will you?

Gellburg What's that?

Hyman You won't be offended, okay?

Gellburg (*tensely*) Why should I be offended?

Hyman I'd like you to give her a lot of loving. (*Fixing* **Gellberg** *in his gaze.*) Can you? It's important now.

Gellburg Say, you're not blaming this on me, are you?

Hyman What's the good of blame? – From here on out *tuchas offen tisch*, okay? And Phillip?

Gellburg Yes?

Hyman Try not to let yourself get mad.

Gellberg *turns and goes out.* **Hyman** *returns to his desk, makes some notes.* **Margaret** *enters.*

Margaret That's one miserable little pisser.*

Hyman *writes, doesn't look up.*

Margaret He's a dictator, you know. I was just remembering when I went to the grandmother's funeral? He stands outside the funeral parlour and decides who's going to sit with who in the limousines for the cemetery. 'You sit with him, you sit with her . . . ' And they obey him like he owned the funeral!

Hyman Did you find out what's playing?

Margaret At the Beverly they've got Ginger Rogers and Fred Astaire. Jimmy Cagney's at the Rialto* but it's another gangster story.

Hyman I'm beginning to get a sour feeling about this thing. I barely know my way around psychiatry, I'm not completely sure I ought to get into it.

Margaret Why not? – She's a very beautiful woman.

Hymen (*matching her wryness*) Well, is that a reason to turn her away? (*He laughs, grasps her hand.*) Something about it fascinates me – no disease and she's paralysed. I'd really love to give it a try. I mean I don't want to turn myself into a post office, shipping all the hard cases to specialists, the woman's sick and I'd like to help.

Margaret But if you're not getting anywhere in a little while you'll promise to send her to somebody.

Hyman Absolutely. (*Committed now: full enthusiasm.*) I just feel there's something about it that I understand. – Let's see Cagney.

Margaret Oh, no Fred Astaire.

Hyman That's what I meant. Come here.

Margaret (*as he embraces her*) We should leave now . . .

Hyman You're the best, Margaret.

Margaret A lot of good it does me.

Hyman If it really bothers you, I'll get someone else to take the case.

Margaret You won't, you know you won't. (*He is lifting her skirt.*) Don't, Harry. Come on. (*She frees her skirt, he kisses her breasts.*)

Hyman Should I tell you what I'd like to do with you?

Margaret Tell me, yes, tell me. And make it wonderful.

Hyman We find an island and we strip and go riding on this white horse –

Margaret Together.

Hyman You in front.

Margaret Naturally.

Hyman And then we go swimming . . .

Margaret Harry, that's lovely.

Hyman And I hire this shark to swim very close and we just manage to get out of the water, and we're so grateful to be alive we fall down on the beach together and . . .

Margaret (*pressing his lips shut*) Sometimes you're so good. (*She kisses him.*)

Blackout.

The lone cellist plays. Then lights go down.

Scene Two

Next evening. The Gellberg bedroom. **Sylvia Gellberg** *is seated in a wheelchair, reading a newspaper. She is in mid-forties, a buxom, capable and warm woman. Right now her hair is brushed down to her shoulders, and she is in a nightgown and robe. She reads the paper with an intense, almost haunted interest, looking up now and then to visualize. Her sister* **Harriet**, *a couple of years younger, is straightening up the bedcover.*

Harriet So what do you want, steak or chicken? Or maybe he'd like chops for a change.

Sylvia Please, don't put yourself out, Phillip doesn't mind a little shopping.

Harriet What's the matter with you, I'm going anyway, he's got enough on his mind.

Sylvia Well all right, get a couple of chops.

Harriet And what about you. You have to start eating!

Sylvia I'm eating.

Harriet What, a piece of cucumber? Look how pale you are. And what is this with newspapers night and day?

Sylvia I like to see what's happening.

Harriet I don't know about this doctor. Maybe you need a specialist.

Sylvia He brought one two days ago, Dr Sherman. From Mount Sinai.

Harriet Really? And?

Sylvia We're waiting to hear. I like Dr Hyman.

Harriet Nobody in the family ever had anything like this. You feel *something*, though, don't you?

Sylvia (*pause; she lifts her face*) Yes . . . but inside, not on the skin. (*Looks at her legs.*) I can harden the muscles but I can't lift them. (*Strokes her thighs.*) I seem to have an ache. Not only here but . . . (*She runs her hands down her trunk.*) my whole body seems

. . . I can't describe it. It's like I was just born and I . . . didn't want to come out yet. Like a deep, terrible aching . . .

Harriet Didn't want to come out yet! What are you talking about?

Sylvia (*sighs gently, knowing* **Harriet** *can never understand*) Maybe if he has a nice duck. If not, get the chops. And thanks, Harriet, it's sweet of you. – By the way, what did David decide?

Harriet He's not going to college.

Sylvia (*shocked*) I don't believe it! With a scholarship and he's not going?

Harriet What can we do? (*Resignedly.*) He says college wouldn't help him get a job anyway.*

Sylvia Harriet, that's terrible! – Listen, tell him I have to talk to him.

Harriet Would you! I was going to ask you but with this happening – (*Indicates her legs.*) I didn't think you'd . . .

Sylvia Never mind, tell him to come over. And you must tell Murray he's got to put his foot down – you've got a brilliant boy! My God . . . (*Picks up newspaper.*) If I'd had a chance to go to college, I'd have had a whole different life, you can't let this happen.

Harriet I'll tell David . . . I wish I knew what is suddenly so interesting in a newspaper. This is not normal, Sylvia, is it?

Sylvia (*pause; she stares ahead*) They are making old men crawl around and clean the sidewalks with toothbrushes.

Harriet Who is?

Sylvia In Germany. Old men with beards!

Harriet So why are you so interested in that? What business of yours is that?

Sylvia (*slight pause; searches within*) I don't really know. (*A slight pause.*) Remember Grandpa? His eyeglasses with the bent sidepiece? One of the old men in the paper was his spitting image, he had the same exact glasses with the wire frames. I can't get it out of my mind. On their knees on the sidewalk, two old men. And there's fifteen or twenty people standing in a circle laughing at them scrubbing with toothbrushes. There's three women in the picture; they're holding their coat collars closed, so it must have been cold.*

Harriet Why would they make them scrub with toothbrushes?

Sylvia (*angered*) To humiliate them, to make fools of them!

Harriet Oh!

Sylvia How can you be so . . . so . . . ? (*Breaks off before she goes too far.*) Harriet, please . . . leave me alone, will you?

Harriet This is not normal. Murray says the same thing. I swear to God, he came home last night and says, 'She's got to stop thinking about those Germans.' And you know how he loves current events. (**Sylvia** *is staring ahead.*) I'll see if the duck looks good, if not I'll get chops. Can I get you something now?

Sylvia No, I'm fine thanks.

Harriet I'm going. (*Moves upstage of* **Sylvia**.)

Sylvia Yes.

Sylvia *returns to her paper.* **Harriet** *watches anxiously for a moment, out of* **Sylvia**'*s sightline, then exits.* **Sylvia** *turns a page, absorbed in the paper. Suddenly she turns in shock –* **Gellberg** *is standing behind her. He holds a small paper bag.*

Sylvia Oh! I didn't hear you come in.

Gellberg I tiptoed, in case you were dozing off . . . (*His dour smile.*) I bought you some sour pickles.

Sylvia Oh, that's nice! Later maybe. You have one.

Gellburg I'll wait. (*Awkwardly but determined.*) I was passing Greenberg's* on Flatbush Avenue and I suddenly remembered how you used to love them. Remember?

Sylvia Thanks, that's nice of you. What were you doing on Flatbush Avenue?

Gellburg There's a property across from A&S.* I'm probably going to foreclose.

Sylvia Oh, that's sad. Are they nice people?

Gellburg (*shrugs*) People are people – I gave them two extensions but they'll never manage . . . nothing up here. (*Taps his temple.*)

Sylvia Aren't you early?

Gellburg I got worried about you. Doctor come?

Sylvia He called; he has results of the tests but he wants to come tomorrow when he has more time to talk to me. He's really very nice.

Gellburg How was it today?

Sylvia I'm so sorry about this.

Gellburg You'll get better, don't worry about it. Oh! – there's a letter from the Captain. (*Takes letter out of his jacket pocket.*)

Sylvia Jerome?

Gellburg (*terrific personal pride*) Read it. (*His purse-mouthed grin is intense.*) That's your son. General MacArthur* talked to him twice.

Sylvia Fort Sill?

Gellburg Oklahoma. *He's going to lecture them on artillery!* In *Fort Sill!* That's the field artillery center. (**Sylvia** *looks up dumbly.*) That's like being invited to the Vatican to lecture the Pope.

Sylvia Imagine. (*She folds the letter and hands it back to him.*)

Gellburg (*restraining greater resentment*) I don't understand this attitude.

Sylvia Why? I'm happy for him.

Gellburg You don't seem happy to me.

Sylvia I'll never get used to it. Who goes in the Army? Men who can't do anything else.*

Gellburg I wanted people to see that a Jew doesn't have to be a lawyer or a doctor or a businessman.

Sylvia That's fine, but why must it be Jerome?

Gellburg For a Jewish boy, West Point* is an honor. Without Mr Case's connections, he'd never have gotten in. He could be the first Jewish general* in the United States Army. Doesn't it mean something to be his mother?

Sylvia (*with an edge of resentment*) Well, I said I'm glad.

Gellburg Don't be upset. (*Looks about impatiently.*) You know, when you get on your feet I'll help you hang the new drapes.

Sylvia I started to . . .

Gellburg But they've been here over a month.

Sylvia Well, this happened, I'm sorry.

Gellburg You have to occupy yourself is all I'm saying, Sylvia, you can't give in to this.

Sylvia (*near an outbreak*) Well, I'm sorry – I'm sorry about everything!

Gellburg Please, don't get upset, I take it back! (*A moment; stalemate.*)

Sylvia I wonder what my tests show. (**Gellberg** *is silent.*) That the specialist did.

Gellburg I went to see Dr Hyman last night.

Sylvia You did? Why didn't you mention it?

Gellburg I wanted to think over what he said.

Sylvia What did he say?

With a certain deliberateness **Gellberg** *goes over to her and gives her a kiss on the cheek. She is embarrassed and vaguely alarmed.*

Sylvia Phillip! (*A little uncomprehending laugh.*)

Gellburg I want to change some things. About the way I've been doing.

He stands there for a moment perfectly still, then rolls her chair closer to the bed on which he now sits and takes her hand. She doesn't quite know what to make of this, but doesn't remove her hand.

Sylvia Well, what did he say?

Gellburg (*pats her hand*) I'll tell you in a minute. I'm thinking about a Dodge.*

Sylvia A Dodge?

Gellburg I want to teach you to drive. So you can go where you like, visit your mother in the afternoon. – I want you to be happy, Sylvia.

Sylvia (*surprised*) Oh.

Gellburg We have the money, we could do a lot of things. Maybe see Washington, DC. It's supposed to be a very strong car, you know.

Sylvia But aren't they all black? – Dodges?

Gellburg Not all. I've seen a couple of green ones.

Sylvia You like green?

Gellburg It's only a color. You'll get used to it. – Or Chicago. It's really a big city, you know.

Sylvia Tell me what Dr Hyman said.

Gellburg (*gets himself set*) He thinks it could all be coming from your mind. Like a . . . a fear of some kind got into you. Psychological. (**Sylvia** *is still, listening.*) Are you afraid of something?

Sylvia (*a slow shrug, a shake of her head*) . . . I don't know, I don't think so. What kind of fear, what does he mean?

Gellburg Well, he explains it better, but . . . like in a war, people get so afraid they go blind temporarily. What they call shell-shock. But once they feel safer it goes away.

Sylvia What about the tests the Mount Sinai man did?

Gellburg They can't find anything wrong with your body.

Sylvia But I'm numb!

Gellburg He claims being very frightened could be doing it. – Are you?

Sylvia I don't know.

Gellburg Personally . . . can I tell you what I think?

Sylvia What.

Gellburg I think it's this whole Nazi business.

Sylvia But it's in the paper – they're smashing up the Jewish stores . . . Should I not read the paper? The streets are covered with broken glass!

Gellburg Yes, but you don't have to be constantly . . .

Sylvia It's ridiculous. I can't move my legs from reading a newspaper?

Gellburg He didn't say that; but I'm wondering if you're too involved with . . .

Sylvia It's ridiculous.

Gellburg Well, you talk to him tomorrow. (*Pause. He comes back to her and takes her hand, his need open.*) You've got to get better, Sylvia.

Sylvia (*sees his tortured face and tries to laugh*) What is this, am I dying or something?

Gellburg How can you say that?

Sylvia I've never seen such a look in your face.

Gellburg Oh no-no-no . . . I'm just worried.

Sylvia I don't understand what's happening . . . (*She turns away on the verge of tears.*)

Gellburg . . . I never realized . . . (*Sudden sharpness.*) look at me, will you? (*She turns to him; he glances down at the floor.*) I wouldn't know what to do without you, Sylvia, honest to God. I . . . (*Immense difficulty.*) I love you.

Sylvia (*a dead, bewildered laugh*) What is this?

Gellburg You have to get better. If I'm ever doing something wrong I'll change it. Let's try to be different. All right? And you too, you've got to do what the doctors tell you.

Sylvia What can I do? Here I sit and they say there's nothing wrong with me.

Gellburg Listen . . . I think Hyman is a very smart man . . . (*He lifts her hand and kisses her knuckle; embarrassed and smiling.*) When we were talking, something came to mind; that maybe if we could sit down with him, the three of us, and maybe talk about . . . you know . . . everything.

Pause.

Sylvia That doesn't matter anymore, Phillip.*

Gellburg (*an embarrassed grin*) How do you know? Maybe . . .

Sylvia It's too late for that.

Gellburg (*once launched he is terrified*) Why? Why is it too late?

Sylvia I'm surprised you're still worried about it.

Gellburg I'm not worried, I just think about it now and then.

Sylvia Well, it's too late, dear, it doesn't matter anymore, it hasn't for years. (*She draws back her hand.*)

Pause.

Gellburg . . . Well, all right. But if you wanted to I'd . . .

Sylvia We did talk about it, I took you to Rabbi Steiner about it twice, what good did it do?

Gellburg In those days I still thought it would change by itself. I was so young, I didn't understand such things. It came out of nowhere and I thought it would go the same way.

Sylvia I'm sorry, Phillip, it didn't come out of nowhere.

Silent, **Gellberg** *evades her eyes.*

Sylvia You regretted you got married.

Gellburg I didn't 'regret it' . . .

Sylvia You did, dear. You don't have to be ashamed of it.

A long silence.

Gellburg I'm going to tell you the truth – in those days I thought that if we separated I wouldn't die of it. I admit that.

Sylvia I always knew that.

Gellburg But I haven't felt that way in years now.

Sylvia Well, I'm here. (*Spreads her arms out, a wildly ironical look in her eyes.*) Here I am, Phillip!

Gellburg (*offended*) The way you say that is not very . . .

Sylvia Not very what? I'm here; I've been here a long time.

Gellburg (*a helpless surge of anger*) I'm trying to tell you something!

Sylvia (*openly taunting him now*) But I said I'm here!

Gellberg *moves about as she speaks, as though trying to find an escape or a way in.*

Sylvia I'm here for my mother's sake, and Jerome's sake and everybody's sake except mine, but I'm here and here I am. And now finally you want to talk about it, now when I'm turning into an old woman? How do you want me to say it?

Tell me, dear, I'll say it the way you want me to. What should I say?

Gellburg (*insulted and guilty*) I want you to stand up.

Sylvia I can't stand up.

Gellberg *takes both her hands.*

Gellburg You can. Now come on. Stand up.

Sylvia I can't!

Gellburg You can stand up, Sylvia. Now lean on me and get on your feet.

He pulls her up; then steps aside releasing her; she collapses on the floor. He stands over her.

What are you trying to do?

He goes to his knees to yell into her face.

What are you trying to do, Sylvia!

She looks at him in terror at the mystery before her.

Blackout.

The lone cellist plays. Then lights go down.

Scene Three

Dr Hyman'*s office. He is in riding clothes.* **Harriet** *is seated beside his desk.*

Harriet My poor sister. And they have everything! But how can it be in the mind if she's so paralysed?

Hyman Her numbness is random, it doesn't follow the nerve paths; only part of the thighs are affected, part of the calves, it makes no physiological sense. I have a few things I'd like to ask you, all right?

Harriet You know, I'm glad it's you taking care of her, my husband says the same thing.

Hyman Thank you . . .

Harriet You probably don't remember, but you once took out our cousin Roslyn Fein? She said you were great.

Hyman Roslyn Fein. When?

Harriet She's very tall and reddish blonde hair? She had a real crush.

Hymen (*pleased*) When was this?

Harriet Oh – NYU,* maybe twenty-five years ago. She adored you; seriously, she said you were really *great.* (*Laughs knowingly.*) Used to take her to Coney Island* swimming, and so on.

Hymen (*laughs with her*) Oh. Well, give her my regards.

Harriet I hardly see her, she lives in Florida.

Hymen (*pressing on*) I'd like you to tell me about Sylvia; before she collapsed, was there any sign of some shock, or anything? Something threatening her?

Harriet (*thinks for a moment, shrugs, shaking her head*) Listen, I'll tell you something funny – to me sometimes she seems . . . I was going to say happy, but it's more like . . . I don't know . . . like this is how she wants to be. I mean since the collapse. Don't you think so?

Hyman Well, I never really knew her before. What about this fascination with the Nazis – she ever talk to you about that?

Harriet Only this last couple of weeks. I don't understand it, they're in *Germany*, how can she be so frightened, it's across the ocean, isn't it?

Hyman Yes. But in a way it isn't. (*He stares, shaking his head, lost.*) . . . She's very sensitive; she really sees the people in those photographs. They're alive to her.

Harriet (*suddenly near tears*) My poor sister!

Hyman Tell me about Phillip.

Harriet Phillip? (*Shrugs.*) Phillip is Phillip.

Hyman You like him?

Harriet Well, he's my brother-in-law . . . You mean personally?

Hyman Yes.

Harriet (*takes a breath to lie*) . . . He can be very sweet, you know. But suddenly he'll turn around and talk to you like you've got four legs and long ears. The men – not that they don't respect him – but they'd just as soon not play cards with him if they can help it.

Hyman Really. Why?

Harriet Well, God forbid you have an opinion – you open your mouth and he gives you that Republican look down his nose and your brains dry up. Not that I don't *like* him.

Hyman How did he and Sylvia meet?

Harriet She was head bookkeeper at Empire Steel over there in Long Island City* . . .

Hyman She must have been very young.

Harriet . . . Twenty; just out of high school practically and she's head bookkeeper. According to my husband God gave Sylvia all the brains and the rest of us the big feet! The reason they met was the company took out a mortgage and she had to explain all the accounts to Phillip – he used to say 'I fell in love with her figures!'

Hyman *laughs.*

Harriet Why should I lie? – Personally to me, he's a little bit a prune. Like he never stops with the whole Jewish part of it.

Hyman He doesn't like being Jewish.

Harriet Well, yes and no – like Jerome being the only Jewish captain, he's proud of that. And him being the only one ever worked for Brooklyn Guarantee – he's proud of that too, but at the same time . . .

Hyman . . . He'd rather not be one.

Harriet . . . Look, he's a mystery to me. I don't understand him and I never will.

Hyman What about the marriage? I promise you this is strictly between us.

Harriet What can I tell you, the marriage is a marriage.

Hyman And?

Harriet I shouldn't talk about it.

Hyman It stays in this office. Tell me. They ever break up?

Harriet Oh God no! Why should they? He's a wonderful provider. There's no Depression for Phillip, you know. And it would kill our mother, she worships Phillip, she'd never outlive it. No-no, it's out of the question, Sylvia's not that kind of woman, although . . . (*Breaks off.*)

Hyman Come, Harriet, I need to know these things.

Harriet . . . Well, I guess everybody knows it so . . . (*Takes a breath.*) I think they came very close to it one time . . . when he hit her with the steak.

Hyman Hit her with a *steak*?

Harriet It was overdone.

Hyman What do you mean, hit her?

Harriet He picked it up off the plate and slapped her in the face with it.

Hyman And then what?

Harriet Well, if my mother hadn't patched it up I don't know what would have happened and then he went out and bought her that gorgeous beaver coat, and repainted the whole house, and he's tight as a drum, you know, so it was hard for him. I don't know what to tell you. – Why? – you think *he* could have frightened her like this?

Hymen (*hesitates*) I don't know yet. The whole thing is very strange.

Something darkens **Harriet***'s expression and she begins to shake her head from side to side. She bursts into tears.* **Hyman** *comes and puts an arm around her.*

Hyman What is it?

Harriet All her life she did nothing but love everybody!

Hymen (*reaches out to take her hand*) Harriet. (*She looks at him.*) What do you want to tell me?

Harriet I don't know if it's right to talk about. But of course, it's years and years ago . . .

Hyman None of this will ever be repeated; believe me.

Harriet Well . . . every first-of-the-year when Uncle Myron was still alive we'd all go down his basement for a New Year's party. I'm talking like fifteen, sixteen years ago. He's dead now, Myron, but . . . he was . . . you know . . . (*Small laugh.*) a little comical; he always kept this shoebox full of . . . you know, these postcards.

Hyman You mean . . .

Harriet Yes. French. You know, naked women, and men with these great big . . . you know . . . they hung down like salamis. And everybody'd pass them around and die laughing. It was exactly the same thing every New Year's. But this time, all of a sudden, Phillip . . . we thought he'd lost his mind . . .

Hyman What happened?

Harriet Well, Sylvia's in the middle of laughing and he grabs the postcard out of her hand and he turns around screaming – I mean, really screaming – that we're all a bunch of morons and idiots and God knows what and takes hold of her and throws her up the stairs. Bang! It cracked the bannister, I can still hear it. (*Catches her breath.*) I tell you it was months before anybody'd talk to him again. Because everybody on the block loves Sylvia.

Hyman What do you suppose made him do that?

Harriet (*shrugs*) . . . Well, if you listen to some of the men – but of course some of the dirty minds on this block . . . if you spread it over the back yard you'd get tomatoes six feet high.

Hyman Why? – What'd they say?

Harriet Well, that the reason he got so mad was because he couldn't . . . you know.*

Hyman Oh, really.

Harriet . . . Anymore.

Hyman But they made up.

Harriet Listen, to be truthful you have to say it – although it'll sound crazy . . .

Hyman What.

Harriet You watch him sometimes when they've got people over and she's talking – he'll sit quietly in the corner, and the expression on that man's face when he's watching her – it could almost break your heart.

Hyman Why?

Harriet He adores her!

Blackout.

The cellist plays and is gone.

Scene Four

Stanton Case *is getting ready to leave his office. Putting on his blazer and a captain's cap and a foulard.* He has great natural authority, an almost childishly naive self-assurance.* **Gellberg** *enters.*

Case Good! – You're back. I was just leaving.

Gellburg I'm sorry, I got caught in traffic over in Crown Heights.*

Case I wanted to talk to you again about 611. Sit down for a moment. (*Both sit.*) We're sailing out through the Narrows in about an hour.

Gellburg Beautiful day for it.

Case Are you all right? You don't look well.

Gellburg Oh no, I'm fine.

Case Good. Have you come to anything final on 611? I like the price, I can tell you that right off.

Gellburg Yes, the price is not bad, but I'm still . . .

Case I've walked past it again; I think with some renovation it would make a fine annex for the Harvard Club.*

Gellburg It's a very nice structure, yes. I'm not final on it yet but I have a few comments . . . unless you've got to get on the water right away.

Case I have a few minutes. Go ahead.

Gellburg . . . Before I forget – we got a very nice letter from Jerome. (*No reaction from* **Case**.) My boy.

Case Oh yes! – How is he doing?

Gellburg They're bringing him out to Fort Sill . . . some kind of lecture on Artillery.

Case Really now! Well isn't that nice! . . . Then he's really intending to make a career in the Army.

Gellburg (*surprised* **Case** *isn't aware*) Oh absolutely.

Case Well that's good, isn't it. It's quite surprising for one of you people* – for some reason I'd assumed he just wanted the education.

Gellburg Oh no. It's his life. I'll never know how to thank you.

Case No trouble at all. The Point can probably use a few of you people to keep the rest of them awake. Now what's this about 611?

Gellburg (*sets himself in all dignity*) You might recall, we used the ABC Plumbing Contractors on a couple of buildings?

Case ABC? – I don't recall. What have they got to do with it?

Gellburg They're located in the neighborhood, just off Broadway, and on a long shot I went over to see Mr Liebfreund* – he runs ABC. I was wondering if they may have done any work for Wanamaker's.*

Case Wanamaker's! What's Wanamaker's got to do with it?

Gellburg I buy my shirts in Wanamaker's, and last time I was in there I caught my shoe on a splinter sticking up out of the floor.

Case Well that store is probably fifty years old.

Gellburg Closer to seventy-five. I tripped and almost fell down; this was very remarkable to me, that they would leave a floor in such condition. So I began wondering about it.

Case About what?

Gellburg Number 611 is two blocks from Wanamaker's. (*A little extra-wise grin.*) They're the biggest business in the area, a whole square block, after all. Anyway, sure enough, turns out ABC does all Wanamaker's plumbing work. And Liebfreund tells me he's had to keep patching up their boilers *because they canceled instalation of new boilers last winter.* A permanent cancelation.

Pause.

Case And what do you make of that?

Gellburg I think it means they're either moving the store, or maybe going out of business.

Case *Wanamaker's?*

Gellburg It's possible, I understand the family is practically died out. Either way, if Wanamaker's disappears, Mr Case, that neighborhood in my opinion is no longer prime. Also, I called Kevin Sullivan over at Title Guarantee* and he says they turned down 611 last year and he can't remember why.

Case Then what are you telling me?

Gellburg I would not touch Number 611 with a ten-foot pole – unless you can get it at a good defensive price.* If that neighborhood starts to slide 611 is a great big slice of lemon.

Case Well. That's very disappointing. It would have made a wonderful club annex.

Gellburg With a thing like the Harvard Club you have got to think of the far distant future, Mr Case, I don't have to tell you that, and the future of that part of Broadway is a definite possible negative. (*Raising a monitory figure.*) – I emphasize 'possible', mind you; only God can predict.

Case Well, I must say, I would never have thought of Wanamaker's disappearing. You've been more than thorough, Gellburg, we appreciate it. I've got to run now, but we'll talk about this further . . . (*Glances at his watch.*) Mustn't miss the tide . . . (*Moves, indicates.*) Take a brandy if you like . . . Wife all right?

Gellburg Oh yes, she fine!

Case (*the faint shadow of a warning*) Sure everything's all right with you – we don't want you getting sick now.

Gellburg Oh no, I'm very well, very well.

Case I'll be back on Monday, we'll go into this further. (*Indicates.*) Take a brandy if you like.

Case *exits rather jauntily.* **Gellberg**, *with a self-satisfied toss of his head.*

Gellburg Yes, sir, I might!

Blackout.

The cellist plays and the music falls away.

Scene Five

Sylvia *in bed, reading a book. She looks up as* **Hyman** *enters. He is in his riding clothes.* **Sylvia** *has a certain excitement at seeing him.*

Sylvia Oh, Doctor!

Hyman I let myself in, hope I didn't scare you.

Sylvia Oh no, I'm glad. Sit down. You been riding?

Hyman Yes. All the way down to Brighton Beach,* nice long ride. – I expected to see you jumping rope by now. (**Sylvia** *laughs, embarrassed.*) I think you're just trying to get out of doing the dishes.

Sylvia (*strained laugh*) Oh stop. You really love riding, don't you?

Hyman Well, there's no telephone on a horse. (**Sylvia** *laughs.*) Ocean Parkway is like a German forest this time of the morning – riding under that archway of maple trees is like poetry.*

Sylvia Wonderful. I never did anything like that.

Hyman Well, let's go – I'll take you out and teach you sometime. Have you been trying the exercise?

Sylvia I can't do it.

Hymen (*shaking a finger at her*) You've *got* to do it, Sylvia. You could end up permanently crippled. Let's have a look.

He sits on the bed and draws the cover off her legs, then raises her nightgown. She inhales with a certain anticipation as he does so. He feels her toes.

You feel this at all?

Sylvia Well . . . not really.

Hyman I'm going to pinch your toe. Ready?

Sylvia All right.

He pinches her big toe sharply; she doesn't react. He rests a palm on her leg.

Hyman Your skin feels a little too cool. You're going to lose your muscle tone if you don't move. Your legs will begin to lose volume and shrink.

Sylvia (*tears threaten*) I know.

Hyman And look what beautiful legs you have, Sylvia. I'm afraid you're getting comfortable in this condition . . .

Sylvia I'm not. I keep trying to move them . . .

Hyman But look now – here it's eleven in the morning and you're happily tucked into bed like it's midnight.

Sylvia But I've tried . . . ! Are you sure it's not a virus of some kind?

Hyman There's nothing. Sylvia, you have a strong beautiful body . . .

Sylvia But what can I do, I can't feel anything!

She sits up with her face raised to him; he stands and moves abruptly away. Then turning back to her . . .

Hyman I really should find someone else for you.

Sylvia Why! – I don't want anyone else!

Hyman You're a very attractive woman, don't you know that? (*Deeply excited,* **Sylvia** *glances away shyly.*) Sylvia, listen to me . . . I haven't been this moved by a woman in a very long time.

Sylvia . . . Well, you mustn't get anyone else.

Pause.

Hyman Tell me the truth, Sylvia. Sylvia? How did this happen to you?

Sylvia (*avoids his gaze*) I don't know.

Sylvia*'s anxiety rises as he speaks now.*

Hyman . . . I'm going to be straight with you; I thought this was going to be simpler than it's turning out to be, and I care about you too much to play a game with your health. I can't deny my vanity, I have a lot of it, but I have to face it – I know you want to tell me something and I don't know how to get it out of you.

Sylvia *covers her face, ashamed.*

Hyman You're a responsible woman, Sylvia, you have to start helping me, you can't just lie there and expect a miracle to lift you to your feet. You tell me now – what should I know?

Sylvia I would tell you if I knew!

Hyman *turns away, defeated and impatient.*

Sylvia Couldn't we just talk and maybe I could . . . (*Breaks off.*) I like you. A lot. I love when you talk to me . . . Couldn't we just . . . like for a few minutes . . .

Hyman Okay. What do you want to talk about?

Sylvia Please. Be patient. I'm . . . I'm trying. (*Relieved; a fresher mood.*) Harriet says you used to take out our cousin Roslyn Fein.

Hyman It's possible, I don't remember.

Sylvia Well, you had so many, didn't you.

Hyman When I was younger.

Sylvia Roslyn said you used to do acrobatics on the beach? And all the girls would stand around going crazy for you.

Hyman That's a long time ago . . .

Sylvia And you'd take them under the boardwalk. (*Laughs.*)

Hyman Nobody had money for anything else. Didn't you used to go to the beach?

Sylvia Sure. But I never did anything like that.

Hyman You must have been very shy.

Sylvia I guess, but I had to look out for my sisters, being the eldest . . .

Hyman Can we talk about Phillip? (*Caught unaware,* **Sylvia***'s eyes show fear.*) I'd really like, to, unless you . . .

Sylvia (*challenged*) No! – It's all right.

Hyman . . . Are you afraid right now?

Sylvia No, not . . . Yes. (*Picks up the book beside her.*) Have you read *Anthony Adverse*?*

Hyman No, but I hear it's sold a million copies.

Sylvia It's wonderful. I rent it from Womrath's.*

Hyman Was Phillip your first boyfriend?

Sylvia The first serious.

Hyman He's a fine man.

Sylvia Yes, he is.

Hyman Is he interesting to be with?

Sylvia Interesting?

Hyman Do you have things to talk about?

Sylvia Well . . . business, mostly. I was head bookkeeper for Empire Steel in Long Island City . . . years ago, when we met, I mean.

Hyman He didn't want you to work?

Sylvia No.

Hyman I imagine you were a good business woman.

Sylvia Oh, I loved it! I've always enjoyed . . . you know, people depending on me.

Hyman Yes. – Do I frighten you talking like this?

Sylvia A little. – But I want you to.

Hyman Why?

Sylvia I don't know. You make me feel . . . hopeful.

Hyman You mean of getting better?

Sylvia – Of myself. Of getting . . . (*Breaks off.*)

Hyman Getting what? (**Sylvia** *shakes her head, refusing to go on.*) . . . Free?

Sylvia *suddenly kisses the palm of his hand. He wipes her hair away from her eyes. He stands up and walks a few steps away.*

Hyman I want you to raise your knees.

Sylvia *doesn't move.*

Hyman Come, bring up your knees.

Sylvia (*tries*) I can't!

Hyman You can. I want you to send your thoughts into your hips. Tense your hips. Think of the bones in your hips. Come on now. The strongest muscles in your body are right there, you still have tremendous power there. Tense your hips.

She is tensing.

Now tense your thighs. Those are long dense muscles with tremendous power. Do it, draw up your knees. Come on, raise your knees. Keep it up. Concentrate. Raise it. Do it for me.

With an exhaled gasp she gives up.

(*Remaining yards away* . . .) Your body strength must be marvelous. The depth of your flesh must be wonderful. Why are you cut off from yourself? You should be dancing, you should be stretching out in the sun . . . Sylvia, I know you know more than you're saying, why can't you open up to me? Speak to me. Sylvia? Say anything. (*She looks at him in silence.*) I promise I won't tell a soul. What is in your mind right now.

A pause.

Sylvia Tell me about Germany.

Hymen (*surprised*) Germany. Why Germany?

Sylvia Why did you go there to study?

Hyman The American medical schools have quotas on Jews, I would have had to wait for years and maybe never get in.*

Sylvia But they hate Jews there, don't they?

Hyman These Nazis can't possibly last* – Why are you so preoccupied with them?

Sylvia I don't know. But when I saw that picture in the *Times** – with those two old men on their knees in the street. (*Presses her ears.*) I swear, I almost heard that crowd laughing, and ridiculing them. – But nobody really wants to talk about it.* Phillip never even wants to talk about being Jewish, except – you know – to joke about it sometimes the way people do.

Hyman What would you like to say to Phillip about it?

Sylvia (*with an empty laugh, a head shake*) I don't even know! Just to talk about it . . . it's almost like there's something in me that . . . it's silly . . .

Hyman No, it's interesting. What do you mean, something in you?

Sylvia I have no word for it, I don't know what I'm saying, it's like . . . (*She presses her chest.*) – something alive, like a child almost, except it's a very dark thing . . . and it frightens me!

Hyman *moves his hand to calm her and she grabs it.*

Hyman That was hard to say, wasn't it. (**Sylvia** *nods.*) You have a lot of courage. – We'll talk more, but I want you to try something now. I'll stand over here, and I want you to imagine something. (**Sylvia** *turns to him, curious.*) I want you to imagine that we've made love. (*Startled, she laughs tensely. He joins this laugh as though this is a game.*) I've made love to you. And now it's over and we are lying together. And you begin to tell me some secret things. Things that are way down deep in your heart. (*Slight pause.*) Sylvia –

He comes around the bed, bends and kisses her on the cheek.

Tell me about Phillip.

Sylvia *is silent, does not grasp his head to hold him. He straightens up.*

Hyman Think about it. We'll talk tomorrow again. Okay?

Hyman *exits.* **Sylvia** *lies there inert for a moment. Then she tenses with effort, trying to raise her knee. It doesn't work. She reaches down and lifts the knee, and then the other and lies there that way. Then she lets her knees spread apart.*

Blackout.

The cellist plays, then is gone.

Scene Six

Hyman*'s office.* **Gellberg** *is seated. Immediately* **Margaret** *enters with a cup of cocoa and a file folder. She hands the cup of cocoa to* **Gellberg**.

Gellburg Cocoa?

Margaret I drink a lot of it, it calms the nerves. Have you lost weight?

Gellburg (*impatience with her prying*) A little, I think.

Margaret Did you always sigh so much?

Gellburg Sigh?

Margaret You probably don't realize you're doing it. You should have him listen to your heart.

Gellburg No-no, I think I'm all right. (*Sighs.*) I guess I've always sighed. Is that a sign of something?

Margaret Not necessarily; but ask Harry. He's just finishing with a patient. – There's no change, I understand.

Gellburg No, she's the same. (*Impatiently hands her the cup.*) I can't drink this.

Margaret Are you eating at all?

Gellburg (*suddenly shifting his mode*) I came to talk to *him.*

Margaret (*sharply*) I was only trying to be helpful!

Gellburg I'm kind of upset, I didn't mean any . . .

Hyman *enters, surprising her. She exits, insulted.*

Hyman I'm sorry. But she means well.

Gellberg *silently nods, irritation intact.*

Hyman It won't happen again. (*He takes his seat.*) I have to admit, though, she has a very good diagnostic sense. Women are more instinctive sometimes.

Gellburg Excuse me, I don't come here to be talking to her.

Hymen (*a kidding laugh*) Oh, come on, Phillip, take it easy. What's Sylvia doing?

Gellburg (*it takes him a moment to compose*) . . . I don't know what she's doing.

Hyman *waits.* **Gellberg** *has a tortured look; now he seems to brace himself and faces the doctor with what seems a haughty air.*

Gellburg I decided to try to do what you advised. – About the loving.

Hyman . . . Yes?

Gellburg So I decided to try to do it with her.

Hyman . . . Sex?

Gellburg What then, handball? Of course sex.

The openness of this hostility mystifies **Hyman**, *who becomes apologetic.*

Hyman . . . Well, do you mean you've done it or you're going to?

Gellburg (*long pause; he seems not to be sure he wants to continue. Now he sounds reasonable again*) You see, we haven't been really . . . together. For . . . quite a long time. (*Correcting.*) I mean specially since this started to happen.

Hyman You mean the last two weeks.

Gellburg Well, yes. (*Great discomfort.*) And some time before that.

Hyman I see. (*But he desists from asking how long a time before that. A pause.*)

Gellburg So I thought maybe it would help her if . . . you know.

Hyman Yes, I think the warmth would help. In fact, to be candid, Phillip – I'm beginning to wonder if this whole fear of the Nazis isn't because she feels . . . extremely vulnerable; I'm in no sense trying to blame you, but . . . a woman who doesn't feel loved can get very disoriented, you know? – lost. (**Hyman** *has noticed a strangeness.*) – Something wrong?

Gellburg She says she's not being loved?

Hyman No-no, I'm talking about how she may feel.

Gellburg Listen . . . (*Struggles for a moment; now, firmly.*) I'm wondering if you could put me in touch with somebody.

Hyman You mean for yourself?

Gellburg I don't know; I'm not sure what they do, though.

Hyman I know a very good man at the hospital, if you want me to set it up.

Gellburg Well, maybe not yet, let me let you know.

Hyman Sure.

Gellburg Your wife says I sigh a lot. Does that mean something?

Hyman Could just be tension. Come in when you have a little time, I'll look you over . . . Am I wrong? – You sound like something's happened . . .

Gellburg This whole thing is against me . . . (*Attempting a knowing grin.*) But you know that.

Hyman Now wait a minute . . .

Gellburg She knows what she's doing, you're not blind.

Hyman What happened, why are you saying this?

Gellburg I was late last night – I had to be in Jersey* all afternoon, a problem we have there – she was sound asleep. So I made myself some spaghetti. Usually she puts something out for me.

Hyman She has no problem cooking.

Gellburg I told you – she gets around the kitchen fine in the wheelchair. Flora shops in the morning – that's the maid. Although I'm beginning to wonder if she gets out and walks around when I leave the house.

Hyman It's impossible. – She is paralysed, Phillip, it's not a trick – she's suffering.

Gellburg (*a sideways glance at* **Hyman**) What do you discuss with her? – You know, she talks like you see right through her.

Hymen (*a laugh*) I wish I could! We talk about getting her to walk, that's all. This thing is not against you, Phillip, believe me. (*Slight laugh.*) – I wish you could trust me, kid!

Gellburg (*he seems momentarily on the edge of being reassured and studies* **Hyman***'s face for a moment, nodding very slightly*) I would never believe I could talk this way to another person. I do trust you.

Pause.

Hyman Good! – I'm listening, go ahead.

Gellburg The first time we talked you asked me if we . . . how many times a week.

Hyman Yes.

Gellburg (*nods*) . . . I have a problem sometimes.

Hyman Oh. – Well, that's fairly common, you know.

Gellburg (*relieved*) You see it often?

Hyman Oh very often, yes.

Gellburg (*a tense challenging smile*) Ever happen to you?

Hymen (*surprised*) . . . Me! Well sure, a few times. Is this something recent?

Gellburg Well . . . yes. Recent and also . . . (*Breaks off, indicating the past with a gesture of his hand.*)

Hyman I see. It doesn't help if you're under tension, you know.

Gellburg Yes, I was wondering that.

Hyman Just don't start thinking it's the end of the world, because it's not – you're still a young man. Think of it like the ocean – it goes out but it always comes in again. But the thing to keep in mind is that she loves you and wants you. (**Gellberg** *looks wide-eyed.*) You know that, don't you?

Gellburg (*silently nods for an instant*) My sister-in-law Harriet says you were a real hotshot on the beach years ago.

Hyman Years ago, yes.

Gellburg I used to wonder if it's because Sylvia's the only one I was ever with.

Hyman Why would that matter?

Gellburg I don't know exactly – it used to prey on my mind that . . . maybe she expected more.

Hyman Yes. Well, that's a common idea, you know. In fact some men take on a lot of women not out of confidence but because they're afraid to lose it.

Gellburg (*fascinated*) Huh! I'd never of thought of that. – A doctor must get a lot of peculiar cases, I bet.

Hymen (*with utter intimacy*) Everybody's peculiar in one way or another. But I'm not here to judge people. Why don't you try to tell me what happened? (*His grin; making light of it.*) Come on, give it a shot.

Gellburg All right . . . (*Sighs.*) I get into bed. She's sound asleep . . . (*Breaks off. Resumes; something transcendent seems to enter him.*) Nothing like it ever happened to me, I got a . . . a big yen* for her. She's even more beautiful when she sleeps. I gave her a kiss. On the mouth. She didn't wake up. I never had such a yen in my life.

Long pause.

Hyman And? (**Gellberg** *is silent.*) Did you make love?

Gellburg (*an incongruous look of terror, becomes rigid as though about to decide whether to dive into icy water or flee*) . . . Yes.

Hymen (*a quickening; something tentative in* **Gellberg** *mystifies*) . . . How did she react? – It's been some time since you did it, you say.

Gellburg (*driven along now*) Well, yes.

Hyman Then what was the reaction?

Gellburg She was . . . (*Searches for the word.*) gasping. It was really something. I thought of what you told me – about loving her now; I felt I'd brought her out of it. I was almost sure of it. She was like a different woman than I ever knew.

Hyman That's wonderful. Did she move her legs?

Gellburg (*unprepared for that question*) . . . I think so.

Hyman Well, did she or didn't she?

Gellburg Well, I was so excited I didn't really notice, but I guess she must have.

Hyman That's wonderful, why are you so upset?

Gellburg Well, let me finish, there's more to it.

Hyman Sorry, go ahead.

Gellburg – I brought her some breakfast this morning and – you know – started to – you know – talk a little about it. She looked at me like I was crazy. She claims she doesn't remember doing it. It never happened.

Hyman *is silent, plays with a pen. Something evasive in this.*

Gellburg How could she not remember it?

Hyman You're sure she was awake?

Gellburg How could she not be?

Hyman Did she say anything during the . . . ?

Gellburg Well, no, but she's never said much.

Hyman Did she open her eyes?

Gellburg I'm not sure. We were in the dark, but she usually keeps them closed. (*Impatiently.*) But she was . . . she was groaning, panting . . . she had to be awake! And now to say she doesn't remember?

Shaken, **Hyman** *gets up and moves; a pause.*

Hyman So what do you think is behind it?

Gellburg Well, what would any man think? She's trying to turn me into nothing!

Hyman Now wait, you're jumping to conclusions.

Gellburg Is such a thing possible? I want your medical opinion – could a woman not remember?

Hymen (*a moment, then* . . .) How did she look when she said that; did she seem sincere about not remembering?

Gellburg She looked like I was talking about something on the moon. Finally, she said a terrible thing. I still can't get over it.

Hyman What'd she say?

Gellburg That I'd imagined doing it.

Long pause. **Hyman** *doesn't move.*

Gellburg What's your opinion? Well . . . could a man imagine such a thing? Is that possible?

Hymen (*after a moment*) Tell you what: supposing I have another talk with her and see what I can figure out?

Gellburg (*angrily demanding*) You have an opinion, don't you? How could a man imagine such a thing!

Hyman I don't know what to say . . .

Gellburg What do you mean you don't know what to say! It's impossible, isn't it? To invent such a thing?

Hymen (*fear of being out of his depth*) Phillip, don't cross-examine me, I'm doing everything I know to help you! – Frankly, I can't follow what you're telling me – you're sure in your own mind you had relations with her?

Gellburg How can you even ask me such a thing? Would I say it unless I was sure? (*Stands, shaking with fear and anger.*) I don't understand your attitude! (*He starts out.*)

Hyman Phillip, please! (*In fear he intercepts* **Gellberg**.) What attitude, what are you talking about?

Gellburg I'm going to vomit, I swear – I don't feel well.

Hyman What happened . . . has she said something about me?

Gellburg About you? What do you mean? What could she say?

Hyman I don't understand why you're so upset with me!

Gellburg What are you doing!

Hymen (*guiltily*) What am I doing! What are you talking about!

Gellburg She is trying to destroy me! And you stand there! And what do you do! Are you a doctor or what! (*He goes right* *up to* **Hyman***'s face.*) Why don't you give me a straight answer about anything! Everything is in-and-out and around-the-block! – Listen, I've made up my mind; I don't want you seeing her anymore.

Hyman I think she's the one has to decide that.

Gellburg I am deciding it! It's decided!

Gellberg *storms out.* **Hyman** *stands there, guilty, alarmed.* **Margaret** *enters.*

Margaret Now what? (*Seeing* **Hyman***'s anxiety.*) Why are you looking like that? (**Hyman** *evasively returns to his desk chair.*) Are you in trouble?

Hyman Me! Cut it out, will you?

Margaret Cut what out? I asked a question – are you?

Hyman I said to cut it out, Margaret!

Margaret You don't realize how transparent you are. You're a pane of glass, Harry –

Hymen (*laughs*) Nothing's happened. *Nothing has happened!* Why are you going on about it!

Margaret I will never understand it. Except I do, I guess; you believe women. Woman tells you the earth is flat and for that five minutes you're swept away, helpless.

Hyman You know what baffles me?

Margaret . . . And it's irritating. – What is it – just new ass all the time?

Hyman There's been nobody for at least ten or twelve years . . . more! I can't remember anymore! You know that!

Pause.

Margaret What baffles you?

Hyman Why I take your suspicions seriously.

Margaret Oh that's easy. – You love the truth, Harry.

Hymen (*a deep sigh, facing upward*) I'm exhausted.

Margaret What about asking Charley Whitman to see her?

Hyman She's frightened to death of psychiatry,* she thinks it means she's crazy.

Margaret Well, she is, in a way, isn't she?

Hyman I don't see it that way at all.

Margaret Getting this hysterical about something on the other side of the world is sane?

Hyman When she talks about it, it's not the other side of the world, it's on the next block.

Margaret And that's sane?

Hyman I don't know what it is! I just get the feeling sometimes that she *knows* something, something that . . . It's like she's connected to some . . . some wire that goes half around the world, some truth that other people are blind to.

Margaret I think you've got to get somebody on this who won't be carried away, Harry.

Hyman I am not carried away!

Margaret You really believe that Sylvia Gellburg is being threatened by these Nazis? Is that real or is it hysterical?

Hyman So call it hysterical, does that bring you one inch closer to what is driving that woman? It's not a word that's driving her, Margaret – she *knows* something! I don't know what it is, and she may not either – but I tell you it's real.

A moment.

Margaret What an interesting life you have, Harry.

Blackout.

The cellist plays and is gone.

Scene Seven

Stanton Case *is standing with hands clasped behind his back as though staring out a window. A dark mood.* **Gellburg** *enters behind him but he doesn't turn at once.*

Gellburg Excuse me.

Case (*turns*) Oh, good morning. You wanted to see me.

Gellburg If you have a minute, I'd appreciate . . .

Case (*as he sits*) – You don't look well, are you all right?

Gellburg Oh I'm fine, maybe a cold coming on . . .

Since he hasn't been invited to sit he glances at a chair then back at **Case** *who still leaves him hanging – and he sits on the chair's edge.*

Gellburg I wanted you to know how bad I feel about 611 Broadway. I'm very sorry.

Case Yes. Well. So it goes, I guess.

Gellburg I know you had your heart set on it and I . . . I tell you the news knocked me over; they gave no sign they were talking to Allen Kershowitz or anybody else.

Case It's very disappointing – in fact, I'd already begun talking to an architect friend about renovations.

Gellburg Really. Well, I can't tell you how . . .

Case I'd gotten a real affection for that building. It certainly would have made a perfect annex. And probably a great investment too.

Gellburg Well, not necessarily, if Wanamaker's ever pulls out.

Case . . . Yes, about Wanamaker's – I should tell you – when I found out that Kershowitz had outbid us I was flabbergasted after what you'd said about the neighborhood going downhill once the store was gone – Kershowitz is no fool, I need hardly say. So I mentioned it to one of our club members who I know is related to a member of the

Wanamaker board. – He tells me there has never been any discussion whatever about the company moving out; he was simply amazed at the idea.

Gellburg But the man at ABC . . .

Case (*impatience showing*) ABC was left with the repair work because Wanamaker's changed to another contractor for their new boilers. It had nothing to do with the store moving out. Nothing.

Gellburg . . . I don't know what to say, I . . . I just . . . I'm awfully sorry.

Case Well, it's a beautiful building, let's hope Kershowitz puts it to some worthwhile use. – You have any idea what he plans to do with it?

Gellburg Me? Oh no, I don't really know Kershowitz.

Case Oh! I thought you said you knew him for years?

Gellburg . . . Well, I 'know' him, but not . . . we're not personal friends or anything, we just met at closings a few times, and things like that. And maybe once or twice in restaurants, I think, but . . .

Case I see. I guess I misunderstood, I thought you were fairly close.

Case *says no more; the full stop shoots* **Gellberg***'s anxiety way up.*

Gellburg I hope you're not . . . I mean I never mentioned to Kershowitz that you were interested in 611.

Case Mentioned? What do you mean?

Gellburg Nothing; just that . . . it almost sounds like I had something to do with him grabbing the building away from under you. Because I would never do a thing like that to you!

Case I didn't say that, did I? If I seem upset, it's being screwed out of that building, and by a man whose methods I've never particularly admired.

Gellburg Yes, that's what I mean. But I had nothing to do with Kershowitz . . . (*Breaks off into silence.*)

Case But did I say you did? I'm not clear about what you wanted to say to me, or have I missed some . . . ?

Gellburg No-no, just that. What you just said.

Case (*his mystification peaking*) What's the matter with you?

Gellburg I'm sorry. I'd like to forget the whole thing.

Case What's happening?

Gellburg Nothing. Really. I'm sorry I troubled you!

Pause. With an explosion of frustration, **Case** *marches out.* **Gellberg** *is left open-mouthed, one hand raised to bring back his life.*

Blackout.

The cellist plays and is gone.

Scene Eight

Sylvia *in a wheelchair is listening to Eddie Cantor* on the radio, singing 'If You Knew Suzie Like I Know Suzie'. She has an amused look, taps a finger to the rhythm. Her bed is nearby, on it a folded newspaper.* **Hyman** *appears. She instantly smiles, turns off the radio and holds a hand out to him. He comes and shakes hands.*

Sylvia (*indicating the radio*) I simply can't stand Eddie Cantor, can you?

Hyman Cut it out now, I heard you laughing halfway up the stairs.

Sylvia I know, but I can't stand him. This Crosby's* the one I like. You ever hear him?

Hyman I can't stand these crooners – they're making ten, twenty thousand dollars a week and never spent a day in medical school. (*She laughs.*) Anyway, I'm an opera man.*

Sylvia I never saw an opera. They must be hard to understand, I bet.

Hyman Nothing to understand – either she wants to and he doesn't or he wants to and she doesn't. (**Sylvia** *laughs.*) Either way one of them gets killed and the other one jumps off a building.

Sylvia I'm so glad you could come.

Hymen (*settling into chair near the bed*) – You ready? We have to discuss something.

Sylvia Phillip had to go to Jersey for a zoning meeting* . . .

Hyman Just as well – it's you I want to talk to.

Sylvia – There's some factory the firm owns there.

Hyman Come on, don't be nervous.

Sylvia . . . My back aches, will you help me onto the bed?

Hyman Sure.

He lifts her off the chair and carries her to the bed where he gently lowers her.

There we go.

She lies back. He brings up the blanket and covers her legs.

What's that perfume? (*He leaves the bedside.*)

Sylvia Harriet found it in my drawer. I think Jerome bought it for one of my birthdays years ago.

Hyman Lovely. Your hair is different.

Sylvia (*puffs up her hair*) Harriet did it; she's loved playing with my hair since we were kids. Did you hear all those birds this morning?

Hyman Amazing, yes; a whole cloud of them shot up like a spray in front of my horse.

Sylvia (*partially to keep him*) You know, as a child, when we first moved from upstate there were so many birds and rabbits and even foxes here. – Of course, that was *real* country up there; my dad had a wonderful general store, everything from ladies' hats to horseshoes. But the winters were just finally too cold for my mother.*

Hyman In Coney Island we used to kill rabbits with sling-shots.

Sylvia (*wrinkling her nose in disgust*) Why!

Hymen (*shrugs*) – To see if we could. It was heaven for kids.

Sylvia I know! Brooklyn was really beautiful, wasn't it? I think people were happier then. My mother used to stand on our porch and watch us all the way to school, right across the open fields for – must have been a mile. And I would tie a clothes-line around my three sisters so I wouldn't have to keep chasing after them! – I'm so glad – honestly . . . (*A cozy little laugh.*) I feel good every time you come.

Hyman Now listen to me; I've learned that your kind of symptoms come from very deep in the mind. I would have to deal with your dreams to get any results, your deepest secret feelings, you understand? That's not my training.*

Sylvia But when you talk to me I really feel my strength starting to come back.

Hyman You should already be having therapy to keep up your circulation.

A change in **Sylvia***'s expression, a sudden withdrawal which* **Hyman** *notices.*

Hyman You have a long life ahead of you, you don't want to live it in a wheelchair, do you? It's imperative that we get you to someone who can . . .

Sylvia I could tell you a dream.

Hyman I'm not trained to . . .

Sylvia I'd like to, can I? I want to. – I have the same one every night just as I'm falling asleep.

Hymen (*forced to give way*) Well, all right, what is it?

Sylvia I'm in a street. Everything is sort of gray. And there's a crowd of people. They're packed in all around and they're looking for me.

Hyman Who are they?

Sylvia They're Germans.

Hyman Sounds like those photographs in the papers.

Sylvia (*discovering it now*) I think so, yes!

Hyman Does something happen?

Sylvia Well, I begin to run away. And the whole crowd is chasing after me. They have heavy shoes that pound on the pavement. Then just as I'm escaping around a corner a man catches me and pushes me down . . . (*Breaks off.*)

Hyman Is that the end of it?

Sylvia No. He gets on top of me, and begins kissing me . . . (*Breaks off.*)

Hyman Yes?

Sylvia . . . And then he starts to cut off my breasts. And he raises himself up, and for a second I see the side of his face.

Hyman Who is it?

Sylvia . . . I don't know.

Hyman But you saw his face.

Sylvia (*discovering*) I think it's Phillip. (*Pause.*) But how could Phillip be like . . . he was almost like one of the others?

Hyman I don't know. Why do you think?

Sylvia Would it be possible . . . because Phillip . . . I mean . . . (*A little laugh.*) he sounds sometimes like he doesn't like Jews? (*Correcting.*) Of course he doesn't *mean* it, but maybe in my mind it's like he's . . . (*Breaks off.*)

Hyman Like he's what? What's frightening you?

Sylvia *is silent, turns away.*

Hyman Sylvia?

He tries to turn her face to him, but she resists.

Not Phillip, is it?

Sylvia *turns to him, the answer in her eyes. He is amazed.*

Hyman I see.

He moves from the bed and halts, trying to weigh this added complication. Returning to the bed, sits, takes her hand.

I want to ask you a question.

Sylvia *draws* **Hyman** *to her and kisses him on the mouth.*

Sylvia I can't help it. (*She bursts into tears.*)

Hyman Oh God, Sylvia, I'm so sorry . . .

Sylvia Help me. Please!

Hyman I'm trying to.

Sylvia I know!

She weeps even more deeply. With a cry filled with her pain, she embraces him desperately.

Hyman Oh Sylvia, Sylvia . . .

Sylvia I feel so foolish.

Hyman No-no. You're unhappy, not foolish.

Sylvia I feel like I'm losing everything, I'm being torn to pieces. What do you want to know, I'll tell you! (*Cries into her hands. He moves, trying to make a decision . . .*) I trust you. What do you want to ask me?

Hyman – Since this happened to you, have you and Phillip had relations?*

Sylvia (*open surprise*) Relations?

Hyman He said you did the other night.

Sylvia We had *relations* the other night?

Hyman But that . . . well, he said that by morning you'd forgotten. Is that true?

Sylvia *is motionless, looking past him with immense uncertainty.*

Sylvia (*alarmed sense of rejection*) Why are you asking me that?

Hyman I didn't know what to make of it . . . I guess I still don't.

Sylvia (*deeply embarrassed*) You mean you believe him?

Hyman Well . . . I didn't know what to believe.

Sylvia You must think I'm crazy – to forget such a thing.

Hyman Oh God no – I didn't mean anything like that . . .

Sylvia We haven't had relations for almost twenty years.

The shock pitches him into silence. Now he doesn't know what or who to believe.

Hyman Twenty . . . ?

Sylvia Just after Jerome was born.

Hyman I just . . . I don't know what to say, Sylvia.

Sylvia You never heard of it before with people?

Hyman Yes, but not when they're as young as you.

Sylvia You might be surprised.

Hyman What was it, another woman, or what?

Sylvia Oh no.

Hyman Then what happened?

Sylvia I don't know, I never understood it. He just couldn't anymore.

She tries to read his reaction; **Hyman** *doesn't face her directly.*

Sylvia You believe me, don't you?

Hyman Of course I do. But why would he invent a story like that?

Sylvia (*incredulously*) I can't imagine . . . Could he be trying to . . . (*Breaks off.*)

Hyman What?

Sylvia . . . Make you think I've gone crazy?

Hyman No, you mustn't believe that. I think maybe . . . you see, he mentioned my so-called reputation with women, and maybe he was just trying to look . . . I don't know – competitive. How did this start? Was there some reason?

Sylvia I think I made one mistake. He hadn't come near me for like – I don't remember anymore – a month maybe; and I was so young . . . a man to me was so much stronger that I couldn't imagine I could . . . you know, hurt him like that.

Hyman Like what?

Sylvia Well . . . (*Small laugh.*) I was so stupid, I'm still ashamed of it . . . I mentioned it to my father – who loved Phillip – and he took him aside and tried to suggest a doctor. I should never have mentioned it, it was a terrible mistake. For a while I thought we'd have to have a divorce . . . it was months before he could say good morning he was so furious. I finally got him to go with me to Rabbi Steiner,* but he just sat there like a . . . (**Sylvia** *sighs, shakes her head.*) – I don't know, I guess you just gradually give up and it closes over you like a grave. But I can't help it, I still pity him; because I know how it tortures him, it's like a snake eating into his heart . . . I mean it's not as though he doesn't like me, he does, I know it. – Or do you think so?

Hyman He says you're his whole life.

She is staring, shaking her head, stunned.

Sylvia (*with bitter irony*) His whole life! Poor Phillip.

Hyman I've been talking to a friend of mine in the hospital, a psychiatrist. I want your permission to bring him in; I'll call you in the morning.

Sylvia (*instantly*) Why must you leave? I'm nervous now. Can't you talk to me a few minutes? I have some yeast cake. I'll make fresh coffee

Hyman I'd love to stay but Margaret'll be upset with me.

Sylvia Oh. Well, call her! Ask her to come over too.

Hyman No-no . . .

Sylvia (*a sudden anxiety-burst, colored by her feminine disappointment*) For God's sake, why not!

Hyman She thinks something's going on with us.

Sylvia (*pleased surprise – and worriedly*) Oh!

Hyman I'll be in touch tomorrow . . .

Sylvia Couldn't you just be here when he comes? I'm nervous. Please. Just be here when he comes. (*Her anxiety forces him back down on the bed. She takes his hand.*)

Hyman You don't think he'd do something, do you?

Sylvia I've never known him so angry. – And I think there's also some trouble with Mr Case. Phillip can hit, you know. (*Shakes her head.*) God, everything's so mixed up! (*Pause.* **Sylvia** *sits there shaking her head, then lifts the newspaper.*) But I don't understand – they write that the Germans are starting to pick up Jews right off the street and putting them into . . .

Hymen (*impatience*) Now Sylvia, I told you . . .

Sylvia But you say they were such nice people – how could they change like this!

Hyman This will all pass, Sylvia! German music and literature is some of the greatest in the world; it's impossible for those people to suddenly change into thugs like this.* So you ought to have more confidence, you see? – I mean in general, in life, in people.

Sylvia *stares at him, becoming transformed.*

Hyman What are you telling me? Just say what you're thinking right now.

Sylvia (*struggling*) I . . . I . . .

Hyman Don't be frightened, just say it.

Sylvia (*she has become terrified*) You.

Hyman Me! What about me?

Sylvia How could you believe I forgot we had relations?

Hymen (*her persistent intensity unnerving him*) Now stop that! I was only trying to understand what is happening.

Sylvia Yes. And what? What is happening?

Hymen (*forcefully, contained*) What are you trying to tell me?

Sylvia Well . . . what . . .

Everything is flying apart for her; she lifts the edge of the newspaper; the focus is clearly far wider than this room. An unbearable anxiety . . .

What is going to become of us?*

Hymen (*indicating the paper*) – But what has Germany got to do with it . . . ?

Sylvia (*shouting; his incomprehension dangerous*) But how can those nice people go out and pick Jews off the street in the middle of a big city like that, and nobody stops them . . . ?

Hyman You mean that *I've* changed? Is that it?

Sylvia I don't know . . . one minute you say you like me and then you turn around and I'm . . .*

Hyman Listen, I simply must call in somebody . . .

Sylvia No! You could help me if you believed me!

Hymen (*his spine tingling with her fear; a shout*) I do believe you!

Sylvia No! – You're not going to put me away somewhere!

Hymen (*a horrified shout*) Now you stop being ridiculous!

Sylvia But . . . but what . . . what . . . (*Gripping her head; his uncertainty terrifying her.*) What will become of us!

Hymen (*unnerved*) Now stop it – you are confusing two things . . . !

Sylvia But . . . from now on . . . you mean if a Jew walks out of his house, do they arrest him . . . ?

Hyman I'm telling you this won't last.

Sylvia (*with a weird, blind, violent persistence*) But what do they do with them?

Hyman I don't know! I'm out of my depth! I can't help you!

Sylvia But why don't they run out of the country! What is the matter with those people! Don't you understand . . . ? (*Screaming.*) . . . This is an *emergency*! They are beating up little children! What if they kill those children! Where is Roosevelt! Where is England! You've got to do something before they murder us all!*

Sylvia *takes a step off the edge of the bed in an hysterical attempt to reach* **Hyman** *and the power he represents, collapses on the floor before he can catch her. Trying to rouse her from her faint . . .*

Hyman Sylvia? Sylvia!

Gellberg *enters.*

Gellburg What happened!

Hyman Run cold water on a towel!

Gellburg What happened!

Hyman Do it, goddamn you!

Gellberg *rushes out.*

Hyman Sylvia – oh good, that's it, keep looking at me, that's it, keep your eyes open.

He lifts her up on to the bed as **Gellberg** *hurries in with a towel.* **Gellberg** *gives it to* **Hyman** *who presses it on to her forehead and the back of her neck.*

Hyman There we are, that's better, how do you feel, can you speak? You want to sit up? Come.

He helps her to sit up. She looks around and then at **Gellberg**.

Gellburg (*to* **Hyman**) Did *she* call *you*?

Hymen (*hesitates; and in an angry tone . . .*) Well, no, to tell the truth.

Gellburg Then what are you doing here?

Hyman I stopped by, I was worried about her.

Gellburg You were worried about her. Why were you worried about her?

Hymen (*anger is suddenly sweeping him*) Because she is desperate to be loved.

Gellburg (*off guard, astonished*) You don't say!

Hyman Yes, I do say. (*To her.*) I want you to try to move your legs. Try it.

Sylvia *tries; nothing happens.*

Hyman I'll be at home if you need me; don't be afraid to call any time. We'll talk about this more tomorrow. Good night.

Sylvia (*faintly, afraid*) Good night.

Hyman *gives* **Gellberg** *a quick, outraged glance,* **Hyman** *leaves.*

Gellburg (*reaching for his authority*) That's some attitude he's got, ordering me around like that. I'm going to see about getting somebody else tomorrow. Jersey seems to get further and further away, I'm exhausted.

Sylvia I almost started walking.

Gellburg What are you talking about?

Sylvia For a minute. I don't know what happened, my strength started to come back.

Gellburg I knew it! I told you you could! Try it again, come.

Sylvia (*she tries to raise her legs*) I can't now.

Gellburg Why not! Come, this is wonderful . . . ! (*Reaches for her.*)

Sylvia Phillip listen . . . I don't want to change, I want Hyman.

Gellburg (*his purse-mouthed grin*) What's so good about him? – You're still laying there, practically dead to the world.

Sylvia He helped me get up, I don't know why. I feel he can get me walking again.

Gellburg Why does it have to be him?

Sylvia Because I can talk to him! I want *him.* (*An outbreak.*) And I don't want to discuss it again!

Gellburg Well, we'll see.

Sylvia We will not see!

Gellburg What's this tone of voice?

Sylvia (*trembling out of control*) It's a Jewish woman's tone of voice!

Gellburg A Jewish woman . . . ! What are you talking about, are you crazy?

Sylvia Don't you call me crazy, Phillip! I'm talking about it! They are smashing windows and beating children! I am talking about it! (*Screams at* **Gellberg**.) I am talking about it, Phillip!

She grips her head in her confusion. He is stock still; horrified, fearful.

Gellburg What . . . 'beating children'?

Sylvia Never mind. Don't sleep with me again.*

Gellburg How can you say that to me?

Sylvia I can't bear it. You give me terrible dreams. I'm sorry, Phillip. Maybe in a while but not now.

Gellburg Sylvia, you will kill me if we can't be together.

Sylvia You told him we had relations?

Gellburg (*beginning to weep*) Don't, Sylvia . . .

Sylvia You little liar! – You want him to think I'm crazy? Is that it? (*Now she breaks into weeping.*)

Gellburg No! It just . . . it came out, I didn't know what I was saying!

Sylvia *That I forgot we had relations?! Phillip?*

Gellburg Stop that! Don't say any more.

Sylvia I'm going to say anything I want to.

Gellburg (*weeping*) You will kill me . . . !

They are silent for a moment.

Sylvia What I did with my life! Out of ignorance. Out of not wanting to shame you in front of other people. A whole life. Gave it away like a couple of pennies – I took better care of my shoes. (*Turns to him.*) – You want to talk to me about it now? Take me seriously, Phillip. What happened? I know it's all you ever thought about, isn't that true? *What happened?* Just so I'll know.

A long pause.

Gellburg I'm ashamed to mention it. It's ridiculous.

Sylvia What are you talking about?

Gellburg It was a mistake. But I was ignorant, I couldn't help myself. – When you said you wanted to go back to the firm.

Sylvia What are you talking about? – When?

Gellburg When you had Jerome . . . and suddenly you didn't want to keep the house anymore.

Sylvia And? – You didn't want me to go back to business,* so I didn't. (*He doesn't speak; her rage an inch below.*) Well, what? I didn't, did I?

Gellburg You held it against me, having to stay home, you know you did. You've probably forgotten, but not a day passed, not a person could come into this house that you didn't keep saying how wonderful and interesting it used to be for you in business. You never forgave me, Sylvia. (*She evades his gaze.*) So whenever I . . . when I started to touch you, I felt that.

Sylvia You felt what?

Gellburg That you didn't want me to be the man here. And then, on top of that when you didn't want any more children everything inside me just dried up. And maybe it was also that to me it was a miracle you ever married me in the first place.

Sylvia You mean your face? (*He turns slightly.*) What have you got against your face? A Jew can have a Jewish face.

Pause.

Gellburg I can't help my thoughts, nobody can . . . I admit it was a mistake, I tried a hundred times to talk to you, but I couldn't. I kept waiting for myself to change. Or you. And then we got to where it didn't seem to matter anymore. So I left it that way. And I couldn't change anything anymore.

Pause.

Sylvia This is a whole life we're talking about.

Gellburg But couldn't we . . . if I taught you to drive and you could go anywhere you liked . . . Or maybe you could find a job you liked . . . ? (**Sylvia** *is staring ahead.*) We have to sleep together.

Sylvia No.

Gellburg (*drops to his knees beside the bed, his arms spreading awkwardly over her covered body*) How can this be? (**Sylvia** *is motionless.*) Sylvia? (*Pause.*) Do you want to kill me?

Sylvia *is staring ahead,* **Gellberg** *is weeping, shouting . . .*

Gellburg Is that it! Speak to me!

Sylvia*'s face is blank, unreadable. He buries his face in the covers, weeping helplessly, and she at last reaches out in pity toward the top of his head, and as her hand almost touches . . .*

Blackout.

The cellist plays and the music falls away.

Scene Nine

Case*'s office.* **Gellberg** *seated alone.* **Case** *enters, shuffling through a handful of mail.* **Gellberg** *has gotten to his feet.* **Case***'s manner is cold; barely glances up from his mail.*

Case Good morning, Gellberg.

Gellburg Good morning, Mr Case.

Case I understand you wish to see me.

Gellburg There was just something I felt I should say.

Case Certainly.

He goes to a chair and sits.

Yes?

Gellburg It's just that I would never in this world do anything against you or Brooklyn Guarantee. I don't have to tell you, it's the only place I've ever worked in my life. My whole life is here. I'm more proud of this company than almost anything except my own son. What I'm trying to say is that this whole business with Wanamaker's was only because I didn't want to leave a stone unturned. Two or three years from now I didn't want you waking up one morning and Wanamaker's is gone and there you are paying New York taxes* on a building in the middle of a dying neighborhood.

Case *lets him hang there.* **Gellberg** *begins to get flustered.*

Gellburg Frankly, I don't even remember what this whole thing was about. I feel I've lost some of your confidence, and it's . . . well, it's unfair, I feel.

Case I understand.

Gellburg (*he waits, but that's it*) But . . . but don't you believe me?

Case I think I do.

Gellburg But . . . you seem to be . . . you don't seem . . .

Case The fact remains that I've lost the building.

Gellburg But are you . . . I mean you're not still thinking that I had something going on with Allen Kershowitz, are you?

Case Put it this way – I hope as time goes on that my old confidence will return. That's about as far as I can go, and I don't think you can blame me, can you? (*He stands.*)

Gellburg (*despite himself his voice rises*) But how can I work if you're this way? I mean you have to trust a man, don't you?

Case (*begins to indicate he must leave*) I'll have to ask you to –

Gellburg I don't deserve this! This is not fair, Mr Case! I had nothing to do with Allen Kershowitz! I hardly know the man! And the little I do know I don't even like him, I'd certainly never get into a deal with him, for God's sake! This is . . . this whole thing is . . . (*Exploding.*) I don't understand it, what is happening, what the hell is happening, what have I got to do with Allen Kershowitz, just because he's also a Jew?*

Case (*incredulously and angering*) What? What on earth are you talking about!

Gellburg Excuse me. I didn't mean that.

Case I don't understand . . . how could you say a thing like that!

Gellburg Please. I don't feel well, excuse me.

Gellberg *takes a step to leave and goes to his knees, clutching his chest, trying to breathe, his face reddening.*

Case What is it? Gellburg? (**Case** *springs up and goes to the periphery.*) Call an ambulance! Hurry, for God's sake! (*He rushes out, shouting.*) Quick, get a doctor! It's Gellburg! Gellburg has collapsed!

Gellberg *remains on his hands and knees trying to keep from falling over, gasping.*

Blackout.

The cellist plays and the music falls away.

Scene Ten

Sylvia *in wheelchair,* **Margaret** *and* **Harriet** *seated on either side of her.* **Sylvia** *is sipping a cup of cocoa.*

Harriet He's really amazing, after such an attack.

Margaret The heart is a muscle; muscles can recover sometimes.*

Harriet I still can't understand how they let him out of the hospital so soon.

Margaret He has a will of iron. But it may be just as well for him here.

Sylvia He wants to die here.

Margaret No one can know, he can live a long time.

Sylvia (*handing her the cup*) Thanks. I haven't drunk cocoa in years.

Margaret I find it soothes the nerves.

Sylvia (*with a slight ironical edge*) He wants to be here so we can have a talk, that's what it is. (*Shakes her head.*) How stupid it all is; you keep putting everything off like you're going to live a thousand years. But we're like those little flies – born in the morning, fly around for a day till it gets dark – and bye-bye.

Harriet Well, it takes time to learn things.

Sylvia There's nothing I know now that I didn't know twenty years ago. I just didn't say it. Help me! I want to go to him.

Margaret Wait till Harry says it's all right.

Harriet Sylvia, please – let the doctor decide.

Margaret I hope you're not blaming yourself.

Harriet It could happen to anybody – (*To* **Margaret**.) our father, for instance – laid down for his nap one afternoon and never woke up. (*To* **Sylvia**.) Remember?

Sylvia (*a wan smile, nods*) He was the same way all his life – never wanted to trouble anybody.

Harriet And just the day before he went and bought a new bathing suit. And an amber holder for his cigar. (*To* **Sylvia**.) – She's right, you mustn't start blaming yourself.

Sylvia (*a shrug*) What's the difference? (*Sighs tiredly – stares. Basically to* **Margaret**.) The trouble, you see, was that Phillip always thought he was supposed to be the Rock of Gibraltar.* Like nothing could ever bother him. Supposedly. But I knew a couple of months after we got married that he . . . he was making it all up. In fact, I thought I was stronger than him. But what can you do? You swallow it and make believe you're weaker. And after a while you can't find a true word to put in your mouth. And now I end up useless to him (*Starting to weep.*) just when he needs me!

Harriet (*distressed, stands*) I'm making a gorgeous pot-roast, can I bring some over?

Sylvia Thanks, Flora's going to cook something.

Harriet I'll call you later, try to rest. (*Moves to leave, halts, unable to hold back.*) I refuse to believe that you're blaming yourself for this. How can people start saying what they know? – there wouldn't be two marriages left in Brooklyn! (*Nearly overcome.*) It's ridiculous! – you're the best wife he could have had! – better!

She hurries out. Pause.

Margaret I worked in the pediatric ward* for a couple of years. And sometimes we'd have thirty or forty babies in there at the same time. A day or two old and they've already got a personality; this one lays there stiff as a mummy . . . (*Mimes a mummy, hands closed in fists.*) a regular banker. The next one is throwing himself all over the place . . . (*Wildly flinging her arms.*) happy as a young horse. The next one is Miss Dreary, already worried about her hemline drooping. And how could it be otherwise – each one has twenty thousand years of the human race backed up behind him and you expect to change him?

Sylvia So what does that mean? How do you live?

Margaret You draw your cards face down;* you turn them over and do your best with the hand you got. What else is there, my dear? What else can there be?

Sylvia (*staring ahead*) . . . Wishing, I guess . . . That it had been otherwise. Help me! I want to go to him.

Margaret Wait. I'll ask Harry if it's all right. (*Backing away.*) Wait, okay? I'll be right back.

She turns and exits. Alone, **Sylvia** *brings both hands pressed together up to her lips in a sort of prayer, and closes her eyes.*

Blackout.

The cellist plays, the music falls away.

Scene Eleven

Gellberg's *bedroom. He is in bed as* **Hyman** *listens to his heart. Now* **Hyman** *puts his stethoscope back into his bag, and sits on a chair beside the bed.*

Hyman I can only tell you again, Phillip – you belong in the hospital.

Gellburg Please don't argue about it anymore! I couldn't stand it there, it smells like a zoo; and to lay in a bed where some stranger died . . . I hate it. If I'm going out I'll go from here. And I don't want to leave Sylvia.

Hyman I'm trying to help you. (*Chuckles.*) And I'm going to go on trying if it kills both of us.

Gellburg I appreciate that. I mean it. You're a good man.

Hyman You're lucky I know that. The nurse should be here around six.

Gellburg I'm wondering if I need her – I think the pain is practically gone.

Hyman I want her here overnight.

Gellburg I . . . I want to tell you something; when I collapsed . . . it was like an explosion went off in my head, like a tremendous white light. It sounds funny but I felt a . . . happiness . . . that funny? Like I suddenly had something to tell her that would change everything, and we would go back to how it was when we started out together. I couldn't wait to tell it to her . . . and now I can't remember what it was. (*Anguished, a rushed quality; suddenly near tears.*) God, I always thought there'd be time to get to the bottom of myself!

Hyman You might have years, nobody can predict.

Gellburg It's unbelievable – the first time since I was twenty I don't have a job. I just can't believe it.

Hyman You sure? Maybe you can clear it up with your boss when you go back.

Gellburg How can I go back? He made a fool of me. It's infuriating. I tell you – I never wanted to see it this way but he goes sailing around on the ocean and meanwhile I'm foreclosing Brooklyn for them. That's what it boils down to. You got some lousy rotten job to do, get Gellburg, send in the Yid.* Close down a business, throw somebody out of his home . . . And now to accuse me . . .

Hyman But is all this news to you? That's the system,* isn't it?

Gellburg But to accuse me of double-crossing the *company*! That is absolutely unfair . . . it was like a hammer between the eyes. I mean to me Brooklyn Guarantee – for God's sake, Brooklyn Guarantee was like . . . like . . .

Hyman You're getting too excited, Phillip . . . come on now. (*Changing the subject.*) – I understand your son is coming back from the Philippines.*

Gellburg (*catches his breath for a moment*) . . . She show you his telegram? He's trying to make it here by Monday. (*Scared eyes and a grin.*) Or will I last till Monday?

Hyman You've got to start thinking about more positive things – seriously, your system needs a rest.

Gellburg Who's that talking?

Hymen (*indicating upstage*) I asked Margaret to sit with your wife for a while, they're in your son's bedroom.

Gellburg Do you always take so much trouble?

Hyman I like Sylvia.

Gellburg (*his little grin*) I know . . . I didn't think it was for my sake.

Hyman You're not so bad. I have to get back to my office now.

Gellburg Please if you have a few minutes, I'd appreciate it. (*Almost holding his breath.*) The thing she's so afraid of . . . is me, isn't it.

Hyman Well . . . among other things.

Gellburg (*shock*) It's me?

Hyman I think so . . . partly.

Gellberg *presses his fingers against his eyes to regain control.*

Gellburg How could she be frightened of me! I worship her! (*Quickly controlling.*) How could everything turn out to be the opposite – I made my son in this bed and now I'm dying in it . . . (*Breaks off, downing a cry.*) My thoughts keep flying around – everything from years ago keeps coming back like it was last week. Like the day we bought this bed. Abraham & Strauss. It was so sunny and beautiful. I took the whole day off. God, it's almost twenty-five years ago! Then we had a soda at Schrafft's* – of course they don't hire Jews but the chocolate ice-cream is the best. Then we went over to Orchard Street* for bargains. Bought our first pots and sheets, blankets, pillowcases. The street was full of pushcarts and men with long beards like a hundred years ago. It's funny, I felt so at home and happy there that day, a street full of Jews, one Moses* after another. But they all turned to watch her go by, those fakers. She was a knockout; sometimes walking down a street I couldn't believe I was married to her. Listen . . . (*Breaks off with some diffidence.*) You're an educated man, I only went to high school – I wish we could talk about the Jews.

Hyman I never studied the history, if that's what you . . .

Gellburg . . . I don't know where I am . . .

Hyman You mean as a Jew?

Gellburg Do you think about it much? I never . . . for instance, a Jew in love with horses is something I never heard of.

Hyman My grandfather in Odessa* was a horse dealer.

Gellburg You don't say! I wouldn't know you were Jewish except for your name.

Hyman I have cousins up near Syracuse who are still in the business – they break horses. You know there are Chinese Jews.

Gellburg I heard of that! And they look Chinese?

Hyman They are Chinese. They'd probably say you don't look Jewish.

Gellburg Ha! That's funny. (*His laugh disappears; he stares.*) Why is it so hard to be a Jew?

Hyman It's hard to be anything.

Gellburg No, it's different for them. Being a Jew is a full-time job. Except you don't think about it much, do you. – Like when you're on your horse, or . . .

Hyman It's not an obsession for me . . .

Gellburg But how'd you come to marry a shiksa?*

Hyman We were thrown together when I was interning, and we got very close, and . . . well, she was a good partner, she helped me, and still does. And I loved her.

Gellburg – A Jewish woman couldn't help you?

Hyman Sure. But it just didn't happen.

Gellburg It wasn't so you wouldn't seem Jewish?

Hymen (*coldly*) I never pretended I wasn't Jewish.*

Gellburg (*almost shaking with some fear*) Look, don't be mad, I'm only trying to figure out.

Hymen (*sensing the underlying hostility*) What are you driving at, I don't understand this whole conversation.

Gellburg Hyman, help me! I've never been so afraid in my life.

Hyman If you're alive you're afraid; we're born afraid – a new-born baby is not a picture of confidence; but how you deal with fear, that's what counts. I don't think you dealt with it very well.

Gellburg Why! How did I deal with it?

Hyman I think you tried to disappear into the goyim.*

Gellburg . . . You believe in God?

Hyman I'm a Socialist. I think we're at the end of religion.*

Gellburg You mean everybody working for the government.

Hyman It's the only future that makes any rational sense.

Gellburg God forbid. But how can there be Jews if there's no God?

Hyman Oh, they'll find something to worship. The Christians will too – maybe different brands of ketchup.

Gellburg (*laughs*) Boy, the things you come out with sometimes . . . !

Hyman – Some day we're all going to look like a lot of monkeys running around trying to figure out a coconut.

Gellburg She believes in you, Hyman . . . I want you to tell her – tell her I'm going to change. She has no right to be so frightened. Of me or anything else. They will never destroy us. When the last Jew dies the light of the world will go out. She has to understand that – those Germans are shooting at the sun!

Hyman Be quiet.

Gellburg I want my wife back. I want her back before something happens. I feel like there's nothing inside me, I feel empty. I want her back.

Hyman Phillip, what can I do about that?

Gellburg Never mind . . . Since you started coming around in those boots . . . like some kind of horseback rider . . . ?

Hyman What the hell are you talking about!

Gellburg Since you came around she looks down at me like a miserable piece of shit!

Hyman Phillip . . .

Gellburg Don't 'Phillip' me, just stop it!

Hyman Don't scream at me, Phillip, you know how to get your wife back! . . . don't tell me there's a mystery to that!

Pause.

Gellburg She actually told you that I . . . ?

Hyman It came out while we were talking. It was bound to, sooner or later, wasn't it?

Gellburg (*gritting his teeth*) I never told this to anyone . . . but years ago when I used to make love to her, I would feel almost like a small baby on top of her, like she was giving me birth. That's some idea? In bed next to me she was like a . . . a marble god. I worshipped her, Hyman, from the day I laid eyes on her.

Hyman I'm sorry for you, Phillip.

Gellburg How can she be so afraid of me? Tell me the truth.

Hyman I don't know; maybe, for one thing . . . these remarks you're always making about Jews.

Gellburg What remarks?

Hyman Like not wanting to be mistaken for Goldberg.

Gellburg So I'm a Nazi? Is Gellburg Goldberg? It's not, is it?

Hyman No, but continually making the point is kind of . . .

Gellburg Kind of what? What is kind of? Why don't you say the truth?

Hyman All right, you want the truth? Do you? Look in the mirror sometime!

Gellburg . . . In the mirror!

Hyman You hate yourself, that's what's scaring her to death.* That's my opinion. How's it possible I don't know, but I think you helped paralyse her with this 'Jew, Jew, Jew' coming out of your mouth and the same time she reads it in the paper and it's coming out of the radio day and night? You wanted to know what I think . . . that's exactly what I think.

Gellburg But there are some days I feel like going and sitting in the Schul* with the old men and pulling the *tallis** over my head and be a full-time Jew the rest of my life. With the sidelocks and the black hat, and settle it once and for all. And other times . . . yes, I could almost kill them. They infuriate me. I am ashamed of them and that I look like them. (*Gasping again.*) – Why must we be different? Why is it? What is it for?

Hyman And supposing it turns out that we're *not* different, who are you going to blame then?

Gellburg What are you talking about?

Hyman I'm talking about all this grinding and screaming that's going on inside you – you're wearing yourself out for nothing, Phillip, absolutely nothing! – I'll tell you a secret – I have all kinds coming into my office, and there's not one of them who one way or another is not persecuted. Yes. *Everybody's* persecuted. The poor by the rich, the rich by the poor, the black by the white, the white by the black, the men by the women, the women by the men, the Catholics by the Protestants, the Protestants by the Catholics – and of course all of them by the Jews. Everybody's persecuted – sometimes I wonder, maybe that's what holds this country together! And what's really amazing is that you can't find anybody who's persecuting anybody else.

Gellburg So you mean there's no Hitler?

Hyman Hitler? Hitler is the perfect example of the persecuted man! I've heard him – he kvetches* likes an elephant was standing on his pecker! They've turned that whole beautiful country into one gigantic kvetch! (*Takes his bag.*) The nurse'll be here soon.

Gellburg So what's the solution?

Hyman I don't see any. Except the mirror. But nobody's going to look at himself and ask what am I doing – you might as well tell him to take a seat in the hottest part of hell. Forgive her, Phillip, is all I really know to tell you. (*Grins.*) But that's the easy part – I speak from experience.

Gellburg What's the hard part?

Hyman To forgive yourself, I guess. And the Jews. And while you're at it, you can throw in the goyim. Best thing for the heart you know.

Hyman *exits.* **Gellberg** *stares into space.*

Sylvia *enters,* **Margaret** *pushing the chair.*

Margaret I'll leave you now, Sylvia.

Sylvia Thanks for sitting with me.

Gellburg (*a little wave of the hand*) Thank you, Mrs Hyman!

Margaret I think your color's coming back a little.

Gellburg Well, I've been running around the block.

Margaret (*a burst of laughter and shaking her finger at him*) I always knew there was a sense of humor somewhere inside that black suit!

Gellburg Yes, well . . . I finally got the joke.

Margaret (*laughs, and to* **Sylvia**) I'll try to look in tomorrow. (*To both.*) Goodbye.

Margaret *exits. A silence between them grows self-conscious.*

Gellburg You all right in that room?

Sylvia It's better this way, we'll both get more rest. You all right?

Gellburg I want to apologize.

Sylvia I'm not blaming you, Phillip. The years I wasted I know I threw away myself. I think I always knew I was doing it but I couldn't stop it.

Gellburg If only you could believe I never meant you harm, it would . . .

Sylvia I believe you. But I have to tell you something. When I said not to sleep with me . . .

Gellburg I know . . .

Sylvia (*nervously sharp*) You don't know! – I'm trying to tell you something! (*Containing herself.*) For some reason I keep thinking of how I used to be; remember my parents' house, how full of love it always was? Nobody was ever afraid of anything. But with us, Phillip, wherever I looked there was something to be suspicious about. Somebody who was going to take advantage of us or God knows what. I've been tiptoeing around my life for thirty years, and I'm not going to pretend – I hate it all now, everything I did is stupid and ridiculous! I can't find myself in my life. (*She hits her legs.*) Or in this now, this thing that can't even walk! I am not this *thing*! And it has me, it has me and will never let me go. (*She weeps.*)

Gellburg Sshh! I understand. I wasn't telling you the truth. I always tried to seem otherwise, but I've been more afraid than I looked.

Sylvia Afraid of what?

Gellburg Everything. Of Germany. Mr Case. Of what could happen to us here. I think I was more afraid than you are, a hundred times more! And meantime there are Chinese Jews, for God's sake.

Sylvia What do you mean?

Gellburg They're *Chinese*! – and here I spend a lifetime looking in the mirror at my face! – Why we're different I will never understand but to live so afraid, I don't want that anymore. I tell you, if I live I have to try to change myself. – Sylvia, my darling Sylvia, I'm asking you not to blame me anymore. I feel I did this to you! That's the knife in my heart. (**Gellberg**'*s breathing begins to labor.*)

Sylvia (*alarmed*) Phillip!

Gellburg God Almighty, Sylvia forgive me!

A paroxysm forces **Gellberg** *up to a nearly sitting position, agony on his face.*

Sylvia Wait! Phillip! (*Struggling to break free of the chair's support, she starts pressing down on the chair arms.*) There's nothing to blame! There's nothing to blame!

Gellberg *falls back unconscious.*

Sylvia *is desperately struggling to stand and get over to him. She struggles to balance herself on her legs and takes a faltering step toward her husband.*

Sylvia Wait, wait . . . ! Phillip! Phillip!

Astounded, charged with hope yet with a certain inward-seeing alarm, she looks down at her legs, only now aware that she has risen to her feet.

Lights fade.

Notes

page

5 *that new union's pulled a strike*: in the United States, in the 1930s, high unemployment led to labour unrest. Workers attempted to organise unions and exercise the right to collective bargaining, which led to numerous bitter strikes and demands for changes to labour legislation.

5 *Ocean Parkway*: Ocean Parkway, a wide street that extends from Prospect Park to Coney Island and Brighton Beach, and is also a neighborhood located in Brooklyn, New York.

5 *Mount Sinai*: founded in 1852 by a group of Jewish charities and originally named the 'Jew's Hospital', Mount Sinai served the Jewish population of New York City.

5 *Minnesota*: a state located in the Midwest of the USA.

6 *Lithuania . . . Kazauskis*: the town has been spelled in many ways – Kazhiskis, Kasauskis, Kašauskas, Kazusk, etc. – from the time when Lithuania was Polish, German or Soviet (each rule would change the spelling). To downplay his Jewishness, Gellburg says that his family was 'originally' from Finland, where there were few Jews. Margaret, who is not Jewish, asserts that her family is from Lithuania, home to a large Jewish population before the Second World War, later wiped out during the Holocaust. Her point is to 'put down' Gellburg.

7 *polio*: poliomyelitis, a viral infectious disease that often leads to paralysis, especially affected children. Numerous polio epidemics occurred during the 1930s in the United States. Franklin D. Roosevelt, President of the United States during that time, was crippled by polio.

7 *Park Avenue*: originally named 'Fourth Avenue', Park Avenue is one of the main streets running north–south

in Manhattan, New York. It is synonymous with wealth.

8 *scientific idealist*: pursuing or forming ideas based on a scientific method of hypothesis, deduction and controlled experiment, in short the exercise of reason while assuming an ultimate reality based in ideas. For the doctor and socialist, Hyman, this seemingly contradictory phrase suggests a way of regarding the world from two standpoints, a material world and an imagined or ideal world from which present existence can be judged and improved.

8 *Moxie*: gutsy, feisty.

9 *Aesculapius . . . Anton Chekhov*: Aesculapins was the god of medicine and healing in Ancient Greek mythology. W. Somerset Maugham (1874–1965), the British writer of plays, novels and short stories, was very popular during the 1930s; he studied medicine in London before becoming a writer. Anton Pavlovich Chekhov (1860–1904), the Russian writer of plays and short stories. He studied medicine and practised as a physician throughout his literary career.

10 *They've been smashing the Jewish stores in Berlin all week*: This refers to *Kristallnacht* or the 'Night of Broken Glass', two days of anti-Jewish violence that took place in Berlin, Germany, on 9 and 10 November 1938. Nazis targeted and damaged or destroyed Jewish properties, businesses and synagogues.

11 *Kurfürstendamm*: a famous boulevard in Berlin.

11 *refugees*: many German Jews fled Germany because of Nazi persecution. From the 1880s the United States had been a refuge for European Jews fleeing persecution.

11 *Roosevelt*: Franklin D. Roosevelt (1882–1945) was the thirty-second president of the United States. He was in office throughout the Great Depression and the Second World War, from 1933–45. The WPA (Works Progress Administration) was established by President Roosevelt's administration to create employment through public works projects.

11 *mishugas*: derived from the Yiddish word *mishegas*, meaning 'crazy' or 'craziness'.

11 *Republican*: a member of the Republican Party, one of the two dominant political parties in the United States, together with the Democratic Party. A Republican is generally viewed as conservative, or right of centre, while a Democrat is left of centre and generally progressive.

11 *the Torah*: the first five books of the Bible and the books of Jewish laws.

11 *Heidelberg*: a city in Germany, home to the University of Heidelberg, which was known for educating famous physicians. (MD, Doctor of Medicine).

11 *I simply can't imagine . . . Poland . . .*: this refers to Nazi Germany's territorial acquisitions, which culminated in the invasion of Poland, precipitating the Second World War.

12 *Especially for this neighborhood*: few Jewish women had educational opportunities at this time.

12 *Federal Reserve*: the Federal Reserve is the central banking system of the United States.

12 *Congressman*: a member of the United States House of Representatives. A member of Congress is elected by voters in an electoral district to represent their interests. During President Roosevelt's time in office, the Democratic Party dominated the House of Representatives.

13 *hysterical paralysis*: a form of 'conversion disorder', a medical condition in which a person's mental state manifests itself in a physical disorder or disease.

13 *shell-shock during the War*: the reaction of soldiers to the stress and horrors of warfare. From the time of the First World War, it was considered a psychiatric illness which primarily affected the nervous system.

14 *Mortgage Department of Brooklyn Guarantee and Trust*: the department where loans are obtained in order to finance buying property. A bank called the Brooklyn Trust Company (founded in 1866) was located in Brooklyn Heights. Before the Depression, many people took out mortgages but after the economic crash they could not afford to keep up their payments. Lenders took

possession of the mortgaged properties and as a result many people lost their homes.

14 *Tuchas offen tisch*: a Yiddish figurative saying: 'arse on the table'. This common idiomatic expression was heard frequently in card games, often to mean: 'Put up or shut up!' or 'your cards face up' in poker games, political arguments and other such festive occasions. Yiddish is a language spoken by Ashkenazi Jews, of central or eastern European descent which is based on a German dialect, though written in Hebrew letters.

15 *Rudolph Valentino*: Rudolf Valentino (1895–1926) was an Italian-American screen star and a sex symbol. He was a screen idol in the 1920s.

16 *anti-Semites*: people who are hostile to or prejudiced against Jews.

16 *the Depression*: the economic crash that began in 1929 and continued until the outbreak of the Second World War.

16 *foreclosing*: the act of taking possession of mortgaged property when a client has been unable to make mortgage payments.

17 *only Jew*: anti-Semitism was common in the United States during the inter-war period. It affected employment and educational and social opportunities for Jewish-American citizens.

19 *old country . . . Russia*: the native country of an immigrant. Gellburg represents one of the thousands of Jews who immigrated to the United States from Central or Eastern Europe. He is referring to the Pale of Settlement, a region of Imperial Russia, in which permanent residency by Jews was allowed and beyond which they were largely prohibited. This region included much of present-day Lithuania, Belarus, Poland, Moldova, Ukraine and parts of western Russia.

19 *dybbuk*: according to Jewish folklore, the disturbed ghost or spirit of a dead person. There is a famous 1914 Yiddish play called *The Dybbuk, or Between Two Worlds* by S. Ansky, which relates the story of a young bride possessed by a dybbuk. It was made into a film in 1937.

19 *Rabbi*: in Judaism, a religious teacher and leader.

20 *the Beverly . . . the Rialto*: in the 1930s the Beverly was a second-run movie theatre in Brooklyn, while the Rialto was a first-run movie theatre, also in Brooklyn, in the neighbourhood of Flatbush. Ginger Rogers (1911–95) and Fred Astaire (1899–1987) were a famous American film duo, popular actors, singers and dancers. James Francis Cagney (1899–1986), an American actor known for his portrayal of tough characters, was a popular film star in the 1930s.

23 *he says college wouldn't help him get a job anyway*: during the Depression, unemployment was so severe that a university or college education did not necessarily lead to a job. As a result, secondary school and college enrolment dropped significantly.

24 *it must have been cold*: *Kristallnacht* took place in November of 1938.

25 *Greenbergs*: a fictional deli (delicatessen) in the neighbourhood of Flatbush in Brooklyn, which had a sizable Jewish population during the 1930s.

25 *A&S*: Abraham and Strauss, two Jewish entrepreneurs, established a department store chain which had a branch on Fulton Street in Brooklyn, New York, in the 1930s. The store is now owned by Macy's.

25 *General MacArthur*: Douglas MacArthur (1880–1964) was the Chief of Staff of the United States Army during the 1930s. Fort Sill is a United States Army post located near Lawton, Oklahoma, which was home to the United States Army Field Artillery School.

26 *Men who can't do anything else*: many men who were desperate for employment during the Depression joined the army.

26 *West Point*: a United States military academy established in 1802 and located in New York State.

26 *First Jewish General*: Jews held the rank of general in the United States Army before 1938, but this was not well known.

27 *Dodge*: an American brand of cars manufactured by the Chrysler Corporation.

29 *That doesn't matter anymore, Philip*: his sexual impotence.

32 *NYU*: founded in 1831, New York University is a private university in Greenwich Village in Manhattan, New York.

32 *Coney Island*: a residential area, beach, resort and amusement park on the southern shore of Long Island, located in Brooklyn, New York.

33 *Long Island City*: formerly a city, now a neighbourhood, in the west part of Queens, New York. Empire Street is a fictional company. A bookkeeper keeps the financial records.

36 *foulard*: a scarf or necktie made of a lightweight fabric.

37 *Crown Heights*: a neighborhood in the centre of Brooklyn. It hosted a Jewish community during the 1930s.

37 *Narrows*: a tidal strait that separates Staten Island and Brooklyn. It is the primary access to the New York Port and was popular for sailing.

37 *the Harvard Club*: a private club reserved for students and affiliates of Harvard University, the Ivy League university in Cambridge, Massachusetts.

37 *you people*: this distancing and anti-Semitic comment suggests that all Jews have the same (negative) characteristics.

38 *Mr Liebfreund*: a Jewish name that also implies collusion, being German for 'dear friend'.

38 *Wanamaker's*: one of the first department stores in the United States. At the height of its popularity, there were branches in New York and Philadelphia.

39 *Title Guarantee*: Title Guarantee and Trust was a bank in New York City.

39 *defensive price*: a purchase price that protects a property investor from a financial loss if the value of the building decreases.

40 *Brighton Beach*: a community in Brooklyn, New York, near Coney Island.

40 *Ocean Parkway . . . poetry*: the tree-lined boulevard had a bridle path during the 1930s and for many years after that.

43 *Anthony Adverse*: published in 1933, a bestselling American romance written by Hervey Allen. The film version was

released in 1936.

43 *Womrath's*: a rental library. Rental libraries flourished in the United States in the 1920s and 1930s, transforming American book-buying and reading habits. Libraries were often adjuncts to bookshops, but many operated as independent businesses. Arthur R. Womrath developed one of the most significant chains of libraries, charging fees of twenty-five cents a week or more. By 1930 Womrath had seventy-two branches in fourteen cities.

45 *The American medical schools . . . maybe never get in*: after the First World War and into the 1950s many private American universities and medical schools had quotas on the number of Jewish students who could be admitted.

45 *These Nazis can't possibly last*: this represents a common (paralytic) North American attitude towards the Nazis. It suggests that the German people (and the world) couldn't possibly tolerate a Nazi government for long.

45 *picture in the Times*: there was substantial coverage of *Kristallnacht* in the *New York Times* in November 1938. The *New York Times* is a daily American newspaper published in New York City. On 11 November 1938 the front page was devoted to the events.

45 *But nobody really wants to talk about it*: in 1938, many Americans did not want to acknowledge the persecution of the Jews in Germany.

49 *Jersey*: New Jersey is a north-eastern state that borders on New York State.

51 *big yen*: slang (probably of Chinese origin) for craving; here, sexual desire.

55 *psychiatry*: the study and treatment of mental illness, emotional disturbance and abnormal behaviour. Progressive reformers in America in this period believed that mental illness was the product of environmental factors and that it was both preventable and progressively serious. Sigmund Freud, the father of psychoanalysis, also exercised enormous influence in New York in the first half of the twentieth century, but

popular prejudices against psychiatry persisted.

58 *Eddie Cantor . . . Suzie*: Eddie Cantor (1892–1964) was a Jewish-American singer, songwriter, actor, dancer and comedian who was popular in the 1920s and 1930s. 'If you knew Suzie like I know Suzie' was one of his hit songs.

58 *Crosby's*: Bing Crosby (1903–77) was an American singer and film actor who was hugely popular. He was one of the bestselling recording artists from the 1930s up until the 1950s.

58 *they're making ten . . . opera man*: some crooners, like Bing Crosby, were highly paid artists during the Depression era. Here Hyman makes a distinction between the popular musical entertainment that Crosby represents and his own taste for opera, which is typically considered a higher form of music and another signifier of Hyman's link to European culture rather than to the American popular culture in which Jews played a major role.

59 *zoning meeting*: a land-use planning meeting.

59–60 *You know, as a child . . . mother*: Sylvia refers to Brooklyn in the early part of the twentieth century before large-scale urbanisation took place. Parts of Brooklyn remained rural until the 1930s.

59 *I've learned . . . That's not my training*: during the nineteenth and twentieth century the study of dreams was popularised by advocates of psychoanalysis such as Carl Jung and Sigmund Freud. Freud published *The Interpretation of Dreams* in 1899.

62 *relations*: sexual intercourse.

64 *I finally got him to go with me to see Rabbi Steiner*: rabbis, as religious authorities in the Jewish community, also gave advice in matters related to marriage.

65 *German music . . . like this*: this comment refers to many people's disbelief when they became aware in the 1930s that Germany, historically a country of sophistication and culture, had been taken over by Nazis who burned books and committed atrocities.

66 *What is going to become of us?*: Sylvia's statement can be

interpreted on a number of levels. She might be referring to her relationship with Phillip or their future as American Jews in the light of the Holocaust. Or she might be speaking of the fate of Jews globally.

66 *I don't know . . . and I'm . . .*: Sylvia's comment draws a link between her concern about what Hyman will decide about her fate and the uncertain fate of Jews in Europe.

67 *This is an emergency . . . before they murder us all!*: Sylvia conflates the realities of life in Brooklyn and the violence against Jews in Europe. She calls upon President Roosevelt and England to intervene. But the US was maintaining a policy of neutrality, and England had adopted a policy of appeasement towards Hitler.

69 *Don't sleep with me again*: here, share a bed.

71 *You didn't want me to go back to business*: before the second wave of feminism, women were expected to remain in the domestic sphere.

71 *A Jew can have a Jewish face*: Sylvia challenges Gellburg's denial of his Jewish identity by stating that there is no logical reason for a Jewish person to be embarrassed of looking Jewish.

73 *New York taxes*: property rates paid to the city of New York.

73 *just because he is also a Jew?*: anti-Semites frequently assume that Jews conspire with other Jews to achieve their own ends.

74 *The heart is a muscle; muscles can recover sometimes*: This statement refers directly to Gellburg's heart attack. It implies too that the muscles in Sylvia's legs, which have failed her, might recover. It may also suggest, less directly, that her heart and Gellburg's, or their feelings for one another, might be healed.

75 *Rock of Gibraltar*: the rocky promontory on the southernmost tip of the Iberian peninsula, thought to be indestructible, which inspired the saying 'solid as the Rock of Gibraltar'.

76 *pediatric ward*: area of a hospital devoted to the treatment of children.

76 *You draw your cards face down*: card players do not know the hand they are dealt; they must make the best of it, similar to our lives.

78 *the Yid*: an offensive term for a Jew.

78 *That's the system*: the informal 'system' of discrimination against Jews in the United States in the 1930s.

71 *the Philippines*: The United States army occupied the Philippines until the mid-1930s. By 1938, the United States was in the process of assisting the Philippines to achieve their independence.

71 *Schrafft's*: Schrafft's was an American candy and chocolate company with a number of locations, including one in Manhattan, New York City. Abraham & Strauss was also known as A&S (see note to p. 25).

79 *Orchard Street*: a street in the centre of the Lower East Side in Manhattan, New York City, which was home to many first-generation Jewish immigrants who lived in tenement housing. It was also known for discount shopping.

79 *one Moses after the other*: Moses is a common Jewish name, or a manner of referring to Jews.

79 *Odessa*: a major city in the Crimea, a region in southern Ukraine.

80 *shiksa*: a Yiddish word (which can be pejorative) for a non-Jewish woman.

80 *I never pretended I wasn't Jewish*: here Hyman accuses Gellburg of often masking his Jewish identity, but his attitude also hints at defensiveness, implying ambivalence about his own affiliations.

80 *goyim*: a Yiddish word (which can be pejorative) for non-Jews.

81 *Socialist . . . Religion*: a socialist believes in the collective ownership of the means of production and that history can be understood on the basis of scientific laws. It is not necessary for a socialist to believe in God. The Socialist Party of America grew considerably in the early twentieth century.

83 *You hate yourself, that's what's scaring you to death*: this refers to the damage that self-hatred can cause. Gellburg is a 'self-

hating Jew' in that he hates himself for his Jewishness and has internalised the anti-Semitism of the world around him.

83 *Schul*: a word for synagogue, a Jewish house of worship.

83 *tallis*: a Jewish prayer shawl. With the sidelocks and the black hat describes the distinctive appearance of ultra-Orthodox Jewish men.

83 *kvetches*: Yiddish word for 'complaining'; '*pecker*' is slang for penis.

Questions for Further Study

1. Does characterising Miller as a 'Jewish writer' enhance or diminish our understanding of his work? Is it important to identify the author or the play in this way? If so, why? Draw on the text for examples of how identifying someone as Jewish is either useful or counterproductive.
2. What is the significance of Harry Hyman's horse-riding and of his riding costume?
3. When Dr Hyman says that he 'never pretended [he] wasn't Jewish', he implies that being Jewish is what he *really* is; it is not pretence. But where does Jewishness come from? Is it something in the blood? Does it come from a set of beliefs or from practices? If Jewishness comes from what one *does* rather than what one *is*, how is that different from pretending? What answers does the play offer to these questions?
4. How does the play reflect on its own theatricality? In what sense does the play suggest that Jewishness is a construct? Consider Phillip Gellburg, in his suit of solemn black and his obsession with his image in the mirror, both of which evoke the theatrical character of Hamlet, who has 'that within which passes show'.
5. The play concludes with an ambivalent image, as Sylvia rises above her prostrate husband, 'charged with hope yet with a certain inward-seeing alarm'. What is the ethical significance of this conclusion? Does it imply that free will triumphs over determinism in the end?
6. Does the play suggest that guilt is a productive or a destructive emotion?
7. What are the underlying problems of the Gellburg marriage, and how are these problems related to large social questions of how people should treat one another? Gellburg complains that Stanton Case treats him unfairly.

Does his wife also treat him unfairly?

8 Does the play treat Gellburg unfairly by virtually killing him in the end?
9 As a moral allegory, how does *Broken Glass* speak to social and political problems today?
10 How does thinking about issues of Jewish identity and prejudice affect the play's representation of capitalism and the Great Depression?
11 Some critics find key scenes in the plays to be melodramatic. What scenes would you identify as melodramatic and why?
12 Gellburg says that when the last Jew dies the light of the world will go out, but Hyman believes that all religions will be subsumed by consumerism and that people are basically the same. Does the play give more weight to one view or the other?
13 The play portrays paralysis as a physical and metaphorical pathology and seems to advocate some form of political action in the world. What kind of action does it suggest is possible and what is needed to bring it about?
14 What is the importance of absent characters, such as the Gellburgs' son Jerome and their nephew David?
15 How does the play illuminate the tension between the personal and the professional? Consider the particular occupations involved. What is the significance of crossing, or not crossing, the line between the personal and the professional in particular instances?
16 How does the play reflect on anti-Semitism and other forms of prejudice that still exist today?
17 What is unique about the anti-Semitism that Miller presents in *Broken Glass*? How do you think it differs from other forms of prejudice?
18 To what extent is the female figure in this play always in the object position? Does this change at the end of the play?
19 Why does Gellburg always wear black?
20 What are the historical, metaphorical and psychological resonances built into the title for this play?

21 *Broken Glass* has been called a morality play. Do you agree with this assessment and does it prevent it being a moving portrayal of a marriage?
22 Does Arthur Miller see this marriage from a woman's point of view?

ALAN ACKERMAN is the author of *Just Words: Lillian Hellman, Mary McCarthy, and the Failure of Public Conversation in America*; *Seeing Things, from Shakespeare to Pixar*; and *The Portable Theater: American Literature and the Nineteenth-Century Stage*. He is editor of the journal *Modern Drama* and teaches at the University of Toronto.

ENOCH BRATER is the Kenneth T. Rowe Collegiate Professor of Dramatic Literature at the University of Michigan. He has published widely in the field of modern drama, and is an internationally renowned expert on such figures as Samuel Beckett and Arthur Miller. His recent books include *Arthur Miller: A Playwright's Life and Works*, *Arthur Miller's America: Theater and Culture in a Time of Change* and *Arthur Miller's Global Theater: How an American Playwright is Performed on Stages Around the World*.